COALVILLE REMEMBERED

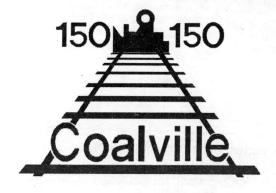

COALVILLE 150 GROUP

Coalville 150 Group gratefully acknowledge the assistance of:

North West Leicestershire District Council
Mantle Community Arts
Mr. Richard J. Willett

Design by June Barras, Brian Barras, Steve Duckworth
Cover design, June Barras
Typesetting by Steve Duckworth for Coalville Publishing Company Ltd.
Laser printing by Mantle DTP Studio

Published by:
Coalville Publishing Co. Ltd, The Springboard Centre, Mantle Lane, Coalville, Leics LE6 4DR

ISBN 1 872479 00 6

COALVILLE REMEMBERED

When the Coalville 150 Group organised the celebrations in 1983 to mark the town's 150th Birthday it organised an open competition for both young and old to present their recollections of the town and district.

Competitors were encouraged to present personal memories or those of older relatives and friends in written, taped or photographic form.

Entries were judged solely on the interest generated and were of such high quality that the 150 Group decided to publish the written entries for the wider appreciation of the public.

It is our hope that these nostalgic memories, so vividly and clearly portrayed, will encourage others to set pen to paper or tape their own memories from time to time. The group will undertake to publish these as well.

We would like to thank and congratulate all the competitors for their initiative and effort in preparing their entries. We present these with a minimum of editorial alteration in alphabetical order of author's name and have illustrated the text with relevant pictures from the Coalville 150 Collection. We would also like to thank Julie Allen for the dedicated work in typing the collection.

The 150 Group continues its work in promoting the proud heritage and community identity of Coalville as it faces an uncertain future. We are confident the people of Coalville and district will welcome this further permanent record of the Town's past.

Denis Baker Chairman (Coalville 150 Group)

CONTENTS

PAGE

1. May Day Celebrations & other post 14-18 war memories.
   Mrs A. Blower

3. Childhood memories of Coalville in the 1940's.
   R. Brown

7. Coalville as I remember it 1895-1914.
   Mrs D. Burton

17. Coalville as I remember it.
   Mrs K.M. Donaldson

21. The Good old days?
   Mrs J. Grewcock

32. My vanished youth.
   Amy Hill

35. Childhood memories of Coalville in the early 1900's.
   Mrs E.M. Hill

39. Memories of John Rowlands Hill.
   J.R. Hill

41. Coalville as I remember it.
   W.J.E. Hill

42. Coalville as I remember it.
   Mrs E.E.G. Holland

44. A Child of Coalville.
   Mrs G. Knight

PAGE

52. Early days of Wolsey Ltd.
Mrs G. Merrivale

53. Letter from Robert Stephenson to his father from Alton Grange.
D. Ramsay

55. Nostalgia.
J.E. Reece

57. Coalville as I remember it.
Mrs D. Roberts

62. Poems - "Old Times","My Charnwood","The Ancient Miner".
R.A. Roome

67. Coalville's first Telephones.
Miss T.E. Stacey & Mr W. Stacey

68. Things I have seen happen in Coalville since 1904.
A.F. Stinson

71. Coalville as I remember it.
F.D. Whitmore

79. Brief Coalville Memories & Memories of Coalville.
Anon.

COALVILLE AS I REMEMBER IT -
Mrs Agnes Blower (nee Frisby)

My family moved to Coalville during the 14-18 war, to a house in Highfields. I went to the Wesleyan School, now Belvoir Road School. Mr Frith was the Headmaster, a very strict Wesleyan who disapproved of dancing. We were very envious of the Bridge Road children who had dancing, especially on such days as Empire Day. We only sang then, very patriotic songs such as 'Land of Hope and Glory', 'Rule Britannia', 'Heart of Oak' etc. For Empire Day we all wore our best clothes as our parents came to hear us sing. If the girls hadn't new dresses, they would have new pinafores -pinafores were always worn then. We sang on the field at the back of the School, if fine. Now it is the Precinct Car Park.

Empire Day celebrations, Bridge Road School 1937.

We envied the Bridge Road children again when May Day came round as they had dancing round a Maypole. However we always had the day off. We took two of the large hoops, crossed them and covered them with coloured crepe paper, paper flowers and perhaps tiny bells. These we called our May poles. We took them and went round to people's houses singing, as carol singers might do now. There were special May songs, like

1

'Here we come a Maying' and 'Gathering Nuts in May'. I can't remember what we did with the few pence we collected. I think this would be in 1918 or 1919.

In 1916 or 1917 I remember a Zeppelin coming over Coalville. It dropped its bombs on Loughborough. My father, Ernest Frisby, was away in the Army during the war, serving in the infantry. He was one of the ex-soldiers who paraded through Coalville on the first Remembrance Day. The memorial, a plaque fixed to the wall alongside the town's station, was bedecked with wreaths and poppies for this parade. A picture shows my sister Phyllis and myself standing with an older friend on the left of the picture. The old stationmaster's house can be seen in the background. The plaque was removed when the present War Memorial in Memorial Square was erected but it is now in the Council Offices on London Road.

In 1919 my father was one of many returned soldiers who attended a Victory Dinner at the Liberal Club on 23rd August. Special commemorative paper napkins were printed for this occasion and I still have a napkin and invitation card.

I was fond of dancing, and in the 1920's, used to go to the weekly dances upstairs at Exchange Buildings (where Electract is now). The dances cost one shilling. Albert King's trio supplied the music. Once a month there was an Open Dance at the old YMCA (where the Health Centre is now) in Memorial Square. Arthur Newbury Choyce, our local poet and teacher, ran these and was the MC, assisted by Fred Forgham who died last year. Tennis dances were popular in the summer when the men wore flannels and the girls white or cream dresses.

However, the Dances that were most talked about were Father Degan's dances on Sunday nights at the Catholic Church in Highfields. Such events on the Sabbath shocked all our parents and I dared not disobey my father by going to them. People came from as far as Leicester and Nottingham. Father Degan was quite a character and kept a monkey. This often got out and I remember what a job we all had trying to catch it when it was in our garden in Highfields.

Our church was the little Snibston St Mary's, but the old

wooden building, St Faith's in Highfields, was used more and, after St James' Church was built in 1933, St Faith's was used for Sunday Schools, public meetings and entertainments. The first Vicar I remember for the two churches was Rev. F.W. Atkins, a bachelor who lived on Standard Hill. The Sunday School Superintendent was Mr Shilcock and I was the Assistant Superintendent in the 1930s. Mrs Abell Smith involved herself with St Faith's a lot and laid the foundation stone for the new St James Church Vicarage in 1933.

After Rev. Atkins, Rev. J.D.C. Wallace was the Vicar, a very popular Minister who was also Chaplain of Ravenstone Alm-houseS and lived in the Chaplain's house there. (This was before St James Vicarage was built in 1933). He was a very friendly person, treating everybody alike. I particularly remember going to Wednesday matinees at the cinema, popular on early closing day, and during the two intervals he would go round the cinema shaking hands and chatting to everyone. This was at the Regal, 4d upstairs and 2d downstairs at the matinees. Mr Wallace always chose to go in the 2d's! This would be in the 1920s. At Christmas he would send cards to all the bus drivers from the Coalville Garage.

CHILDHOOD MEMORIES OF COALVILLE IN THE 1940s - Mr R.Brown

I was born in 1935 and I have childhood memories of Coalville in the 1940s. During this period I lived in and around the centre of the town i.e. Albert Road, Scotlands Drive, Marshall's Row and Bakewell Street.

I suppose most of my recollections relate to shops that were open at the time. The war also played a part, although we were fairly remote from the real action - most of the time.

In the building now used by Burton's as a furniture store on High Street was Coalville's own Palm Court Restaurant, or so it seemed to me as a youngster. A very grand place run by Dunnicliffes, I think, who also sold bread and cakes. Whilst on the subject of food, a "fish and 3 penn'orth of chips" from Stocky's' fish shop was quite a treat. 'Stocky's' stood about

3

opposite Boon's on the High Street, next to the Blue Bell Inn, set well back from the road, as in more affluent times the market used to extend as far as the Fountain Inn, about opposite Curry's. However, for that special occasion. a sit-down supper in Parker's 'Blue Room' was so much better. This stood to the rear of the main fish shop now called 'The Wise Plaice' on Hotel Street. It was a large airy room decorated throughout in blue, with blue wicker chairs and tables with glass tops.

Grocery shops were plentiful. Along High Street there was the 'Star Supply Stores', (manager Mr Turner) (now Boons). The 'Maypole' was next door (now Jones Electrical) where I used to watch spellbound as the manager used to weigh and prepare butter from large blocks using wooden "butter-pats" which left a design on the smaller pound or 1/2 pound portions. There were also branches of 'George Mason', 'Melias' and the 'Home and Colonial'. In Hotel Street, facing the old Baptist Chapel, there was a more "up-market" grocer. Frank Kemp was the proprietor. In Marlborough Square, the Co-op grocery department was where their hardware shop now stands. If, after having made a purchase you required change, the assistant would place your money in a wooden cup, screw this into an overhead socket and by means of a catapult, shoot the whole lot along a cable to a central cash desk where the change would be put into the same cup and then catapulted back again.

Sweet shops I recall best were 'Joblings', about where the 'Times Shop' is now, the 'A.1. Candy Stores' (facing Snushall's) and two others which faced Pickworths, I think the one nearest the entrance to the old Central Field, now the precinct, was owned by a Mr Walker.

There were two music shops: 'Hame's' (where the Greyhound Inn stands) and Ernie Evan's next to Olivers Railway crossing. This was a very large shop and sold musical instruments as well as records, sheet music and radios. Mr Evans had a workshop in Gutteridge Street where he used to repair pianos.

'Timothy Whites and Taylors' had the shop (which is now Woodhouse furnishers) next door to 'Montague Burton - The Fifty Shilling Tailors'. Another tailor's shop, 'Pickerings', stood next to

4

the Midland Bank.

I can just remember the Grand being used as a cinema; during the war years it was used by the Government as a Buffer-Depot, another name for a warehouse I think. I can also vaguely recollect the Rex Cinema being built. Before the advent of Sunday films, the Regal Cinema used to stage concerts with the audience indulging in a sing-a-long to words which were shown on a screen whilst various dance bands played popular songs.

There were two blacksmiths' shops. One, next to where the public toilets are, used to specialise in the upkeep and repair of the miners' long twist-drills. The other one was in the 'Bluebell' yard and he dealt more with shoeing horses.

It seems quite a coincidence that there used to be a branch of the Shire Library in roughly the same place as our new library now stands. Here for an old penny one could borrow a book for a week. I think I am correct in saying that the first public library was in an ex-millinery shop in Hotel Street, formerly owned by two sisters by the name of Broughton. This shop, now selling motorcycle spares, faces the Ford Motors showroom. As a library it was very small and was watched over by a very stern lady whose name, I think, was Mrs Hemsley, a far cry from the noisy place our present library has become.

There was a little pet shop facing the Railway Station, and it had a wonderful smell all of its own.

A few names that might stir memories:- Freddie Davenport who used to deliver milk from a churn, not ready bottled. Mr Vendy, the dentist in Belvoir Road (facing the Little Acorn). Mr Hall, his two sons Alf and Reg, and Pat Ayres, all well known in the taxi and car trade. Jack-o-Bull whose language was almost as bad as that on Channel 4. Bardon Clara, and Pecker Bailey from Marshall's Row who, I believe, held some sort of record for the speed at which he could "fill a ratch" down pit.

There were a few others who were very much a part of the Coalville scene. Mr Marks, who had a fruit stall on the market. Mr Aldread, the Belvoir Road greengrocer, always with the cigarette holder. The Indian gent who used to stand on the market with rows and rows of tiny glass bottles which he would fill with

5

perfume. Mr and Mrs Lashmore, who had a large jewellery shop where the Midland Cycle Co. is today. Bill Randon, who sold underwear. Mr Barratt the cobbler; he had a little shop near the Half-way House. Mr Startin the auctioneer. Onions & Whites, who kept a wet fish-shop on High Street. Mr Haines, who had a sale room and sold second hand furniture etc. This stood behind Pickworths.

Last, but by no means least, two characters who struck dread into my heart at every meeting: 'The Higgins Brothers'. They had a gents hairdressing salon opposite the station, and wore clothes which could have been cast-offs from any Charlie Chaplin film. The worst part of the hair cut was the last bit. Not for them any new fangled brush down. Oh no, one was "blown" free of all those cuttings - not an electric blower either. Theirs was the personal touch, straight from the horse's mouth, so to speak, very wet at times, - ugh, I still shudder at the thought of it.

How did the war affect Coalville? Well, I remember sticking 6d National Savings Stamps on a hugh bomb addressed to Adolf Hitler. This was put on display in the Ford Motors showroom. A captured German fighter plan was put on show in the Central Field. On a clear moonlight night it was possible to see the flack over Coventry. We were bombed. I still recall well the bath hanging from the upper floor of a house on London Road, the crater in the garden next to the Park. I paid 6d to see an unexploded bomb in "Newey's" field (near to where Palitoy's gate house is). If we were quick off the mark when the air-raid sirens went we could share the underground boiler-house with the nuns at the Convent. Otherwise it meant using an air-raid shelter where the St John's Hall is.

One day a train unloaded its cargo of weary troops in the station yard and local people used some of their precious food ration coupons and brought biscuits etc. to share out amongst the soldiers. The very long aircraft and tank transporters used to go the "wrong way" at the traffic island that stood at the clock tower as they were too long to manoeuvre round the normal way. Local people took in evacuees from the London area. I have vague recollections of a shop in Hotel Street being used as the

"Billet Office", though I'm not too clear about its purpose. There were enormous static water tanks in Central Field and a large steel one behind the clock tower.

The building in Ashby Road recently destroyed by fire was, ironically, the fire station. Weird contraptions of wire and metal were tensioned across the large plate glass windows of the rather "haute couture" ladies dress shop in Hotel Street, 'Webbs' I believe, and now occupied by Sports and Leisure. These "gubbins" were supposed to hold the glass intact in case of an air raid, fortunately they were never really tested.

One clear memory from after the war, which now seems a lifetime away, was the little old man who came round with his pole every evening and morning to light the gas lamps in the pre-electric days.

There are many more memories, the more I write, the more I remember, and looking at Coalville as it is today it is difficult to imagine just how much it has changed in forty years.

COALVILLE AS I REMEMBER IT-1895-1914 -
Mrs Dorothy Burton

To look at the ground on High Street where now stands just two buildings - the Library and the Nursery School - one can hardly believe that on the same area once stood ten shops, two public houses, and two rows of cottages! My parents owned one of the shops - Emerton's Cafe - and I was born over the shop on 15th January, 1895. This stood approximately where the Library reception area is now, and indeed covered about the same small area, including cafe and yard to rear! But it was very comfortable and a loving home for myself and three sisters and two brothers. In fact, being three storeys high, in comparison to some of the tiny cottages around, it was pretty spacious.

Our cafe was flanked on each side by the Times Office and Book Shop, the Jones Sewing Machine Shop, Madisons the Pork Butchers, Richards the Tailors, and Radford's Dairy. As a matter of interest, I vaguely remember a fresh faced, sandy haired youngster delivering to that dairy, much later in life he became the round-the-world yachtsman, Sir Francis Chichester.

7

Passing through an opening between these shops, led to Mr Cuthbert, the Blacksmith. He was kept busy shoeing horses and sharpening miners' picks, and the yard rang to the sound of hammer-on-anvil five days a week. Further along, another wider opening was the access to the Cattle Market. This was held on Tuesday, which as you can imagine made that particular day not only very busy but also extra noisy. The auctioneer's box and the cattle pens have only been destroyed relatively recently. I have often been asked why some of the public houses have stables to the rear. In Coalville their principle use was for stabling the farmers' horses whilst they attended these auctions.

High Street then really was the hub of the town, largely due to the weekly market, which extended from the Old Market right up the High Street. Horse brakes lined the street, having brought into town the womenfolk from the outlying villages. Horse transport was laid on by Cherrys of Ibstock, Moores of Whitwick, and someone whose name I don't recall, from Ellistown.

To listen in to the stall holders was sheer music hall. I well remember Lawrence Wright, who later became "Horatio Nicholls" the then well known composer, standing at his father's stall playing a mandolin and selling copies of sheet music. There was also a character called "Sequaw" who dressed like a Red Indian. From his small brake he sold medications to cure all known ailments. He had an accomplice who quite literally "drummed up" business -on a big bass drum! On Friday, the market remained open until 9.00 p.m. with buskers parading up and down. Consequently, the street was as busy when gas lit as during the daytime.

When I am asked "Whatever did you do in those days except work, eat and sleep?" my indignant reply is this. I had a very happy childhood and there was never a dull moment. For a start, there was the Christmas and New Year celebrations which were true Christmas Card stuff! Simple and homely, but very jolly. There were house parties, and in the streets outside local bands played carols. We had three good bands - the Coronation Band (later to become Snibston Colliery Band), the Hugglescote and

Ellistown Band, and the Whitwick Colliery Band. There was no official dance hall at that time, so the New Year's Eve dances and parties were held at schools.

Then, as now, Shrove Tuesday was marked by the making of pancakes. It was also customary for we children to fetch out our whips and tops, battledaws and shuttlecocks. Why, I am not sure, but it was probably because, hopefully, that day would mark a change in the weather! Our games were often interrupted by squabbles as to who had eaten the most pancakes.

Easter was heralded on Good Friday by the street cries of children selling Hot Cross Buns door-to-door from big baskets. It was traditional to have one for breakfast on Good Friday, and their warm spicey aroma was delicious. And yes, they really did call "one a penny, two a penny"! Good Friday then was a totally observed Holy Day, and even the railway ran a limited service.

Undoubtedly, Easter Monday for most was the highlight of the year, for then it was that the annual Track Cycle and Athletic Event was held. This was at the Fox and Goose Ground (now the Scotlands Playing Field). The town thronged with people, some arriving by rail, special trains were laid on from Leicester and all over the Midlands. Others came by horse drawn transport, or of course by bicycle - although a bicycle was considered quite a luxury for most working people.

Competitors were from every part of the country, and when the sport was finished, the streets overflowed with crowds making their way to the Fair which was in attendance in the Old Market and around the Red House, and all up the streets. Everywhere was a hive of excitement and activity.

To a much less degree, though still pleasurable for the children, the First of May was also a day to be observed. Boys and girls interlocked two hoops trimmed with pretty coloured paper and leaves. These were fastened onto a pole, also decorated, around which we then sang and danced. We tried to wear our better clothes on that event.

Speaking of which the annual Sunday School Sermons, or Anniversaries, of the chapels were of very particular importance on the girls and young ladies social calendar! We then acquired our new summer outfits. Although they were very hard times, mothers always somehow managed to rig out their daughters in pretty new dresses, and in fact the whole thing was quite competitive.

Sunday School attendance in those days was a must for virtually every child, and the Sunday School treat or outing was awaited with great anticipation. I attended the Wesleyan Chapel and our treat was held at "Jake Shaw's Field" (now the less attractively named Dog Track!).

Churches and Chapels played a very dominant part in our lives, and there seemed to be a chapel on almost every street. The following were the places of Worship functioning in the era of which I am writing. I can name the organists, but not the ministers since these often only stayed in the district for a few years before moving on.

Organists

Christ Church, London Road Arthur Clarke (blind): Baptist Chapel, Hermitage Road James Starkey: Ebenezer Chapel, Ashby Road Charles Newman: Wesleyan Chapel, Belvoir Road John Rawlings: Primitive Chapel, Marlborough Square Willie Richards: Unitarian Chapel, Bridge Road: Cave-adulam, Hotel Street: Plymouth Brethren, Bridge Road. These latter three were exclusive places of worship, which ultimately ceased to function.

Also the Adult School Hall on Bridge Road, built in 1908, was used for worship and discussions on Sunday mornings. This was for men only and was well patronised. In later years it opened in the afternoons for ladies. I remember a large painting which hung on the top wall titled "The Good Samaritan" painted by the Rev. Kenneth Bond, and presented by Arnold Rowntree of the chocolate family. The Rowntrees still take active parts in the Adult School movement. However, the painting apparently disintegrated with time and was removed.

The Salvation Army were a happy band of men and women who sang and played in the town centre each Saturday and Sunday evening, before returning to their James Street hall for worship.

The Belvoir Road Wesleyan Chapel also had a Day School, of

which I was a pupil. Mr Frith was our Headmaster, a firm but kindly man. If he saw us in the street he would call our name and give a cheery wave, but there was a stern lecture should he see or hear of us misbehaving out of school. An annual outing to Spring Hill Farm, Whitwick, was organised for us. We paid six pence, supplied our own mugs, and gleefully piled into horse brakes belonging to Moores of Whitwick. The teachers came around with wicker clothes baskets piled with bread and butter, and cakes. We had a wonderful time, and on our return journey we waved our hankies and sang "We've all been to Spring Hill and so we shall again!" as though we had travelled to the end of the World and back!

Another popular event was the Annual Flower Show, which was held on the Halfway field. There were four large marquees for vegetables, fruit, flowers and art (embroidery, drawings and paintings, and even handwriting contests). Competitors were offered prizes. A top class brass band was engaged to play on the Band Stand, and the climax of the show was the balloon ascent. The balloon having been filled by the Whitwick Gas Works, at 3 o'clock prompt, two balloonists - Capt. Spencer and Dolly Shepperd - climbed into the basket and released the sandbags. It was a spectacular sight as they soared up into the sky, and the delighted crowds cheered and cheered!

Football was as keenly followed then as now, but on a more local basis. Coalville boasted several first class teams. Each Saturday in season would see several matches with plenty of spectators. The Albions played on the Waggon and Horses ground and they had very good gates as the opposing teams used to bring brake loads of followers with them. There was the Excelsior Club, later changed to the P.S.A. (Primitive Sponsored Association), who played on the Central Ground. They had some very fine footballers between them, notably the Price family, the Lees, Middletons, and others, who have played with top class English teams.

Throughout the year there was a constant stream of entertainments visiting the town. Travelling circuses, led by the elephants which also had to help tow the wagons, escorted by crowds of excited youngsters. Also, there were visiting Boxing Booths, cinematograph shows, and menageries. All were looked forward to with great anticipation. I remember one menagerie offering 5 pounds to anyone who dared enter the lions' den. A jubilant local shopkeeper emerged waving his reward after successfully taking up the challenge. No doubt 5 pounds was as much as he could expect to take in a good weeks trading in those days!

Other visitors of a very different kind were the "Salt Women". They spoke with a Black Country accent, and wore big white aprons over long gathered frocks and linen bonnets. "Any salt today?" they called, and for a shilling you got a very large block, as much as one was able to carry. Of course, houses then often had very long gardens, at the bottom of which a pig was kept. The salt was used for curing bacon and hams after the pig was killed. These women conveyed the salt in horse drawn carts with a hood over in case of rain. Their stocks were replenished from a canal barge, although from which canal I am not sure, but it would probably be Shackerstone.

Coalville has, of course, had its tragedies and the worst must be the Whitwick Pit Disaster in 1898. Although I don't recall it personally, my late husband Ernest Burton lived as a child in the colliery houses, Club Row. He vividly remembered loud hammer-

Whitwick Pit disaster 1898

ing on the doors to waken the householders, who were asked to make as much tea as possible for the rescuers down the pit and on top. His mother told him to go quickly to his grandfather who lived in a cottage in the pit yard (his job being to care for the pit ponies and horses) and enquire where the accident was, since his father was on the night shift. Fortunately, he was later reported safe but the memory of that night stayed with my husband throughout the rest of his life.

As I have said, my husband was born on Club Row, which was one of three very old rows of cottages - the others being Mammoth Street and Stone Row. I imagine they were built when the pit was first sunk, to house the workers. Club Row belonged to the Colliery and was mostly occupied by men with administrative jobs.

The pit banks adjacent to Whitwick pit smouldered perpetually, and although the fumes were pretty awful, they were an accepted part of life. In fact the banks were the means of keeping warm for many an unfortunate man forced "onto the road" in a pathetic search up and down the country for work. Whitwick Pit and its dependant community then was an extremely industrious and active part of the town.

I doubt whether many people remember that there was once a mosaic works near to Whitwick Pit. As I recall, it was called simply the Mosaic Works, manufacturing mosaic floor and wall tiles. It was of some importance to the children as a useful source of off-cuts which served as a substitute for "snobs". As you may imagine, "snobs" was a very popular game in Coalville.

When they finally ceased production, the building stood empty for quite some time, but was later turned over to Nelsons the wholesale fruiterers. The upper floor, however, housed a gymnasium. Incidentally, there was also a gymnasium club for ladies run at the old Eatoughs factory on Forest Road, organised by a member of the Territorial Army.

Coming further down Hermitage Road to the road junction with Hotel Street, on the left hand corner stood the Baptist Chapel which formerly was the "Blue Coat School" - a fee paying establishment. On the opposite corner stood an attractive house with an impressive front porch, bearing a plaque "The School Master's House", although it was no longer occupied by any such person.

Just around the corner, on Hotel Street, stood a row of cottages of which only one now remains. In front of these stood an old village pump, although I don't remember actually seeing it in use, no doubt it was.

What I do remember though are the old street oil lamps. I can visualise the man going around with his ladder, cleaning the lamp glass and filling the vessel with oil, and trimming the wick. It was a full time job, coupled with the actual lighting in early evening and putting out at about 10 o'clock.

Of course, most homes were lit by oil and it was a ritual for one day of the week to be set aside for cleaning, filling, and trimming the lamps. There were some beautiful ornate lamps, which were quite a status symbol.

Turning left at the above mentioned crossroads onto Mantle Lane, the wagon works of Stablefords played an important part in the development of Coalville life. Many people (including my own father) moved into the town as Stablefords expanded in the 1890's, and it came as a very bitter blow when they shut down amongst much speculation, rumour and resentment.

I also remember that Mantle Lane merely had a gated crossing, which caused traffic hold-ups. After some controversy, an underpass was built for vehicles, although there had always been an underground tunnel for pedestrians and cyclists.

Ashby Road once had rows and rows of small terraced houses each side of the Snibston Pit, all of which have long since been demolished. About the oldest property remaining along there now is the Ebenezer Chapel.

Travelling down Belvoir Road there was Sitdown's which was an excellent shop selling fruit and vegetables, flowers, fish, poultry, rabbits and game. Adjoining that was Bert Watters, a gents hat and cap shop. Next was Roughton's the chemist, Myatt Cycles, Allbrighton's pork butchers. Hall's the general grocers, and Greasley's hairdressers which occupied two shops.

Next was an entry to the back of the cottage which was

14

occupied by the Salvation Army Captain, the only remaining house in the row, since all the others had by then been turned into shops. These were Moss the jewellers, Holmes the herbalist, Miss Bancroft the milliner, Vendy the dentist, and finally the cottage where Oliver lived who controlled the crossing gates (hence "Oliver's crossing" as it is still referred to).

Now we come to the entrance to the Central Football Ground. Most of these shops were pulled down to make way for the Precinct. However, the Trustee Bank as it is now, was once the Primitive Chapel and I remember going there with Mr and Mrs Richards to the Sunday evening service when only about 5 years old. Later they built the chapel in Marlborough Square.

Over Oliver's crossing we come to the site of the Nat West Bank, which at that time was a walled-in garden and adjoining shop belonging to Mr Hickling. I must say that the next lot of shops have changed very little, and although I don't remember all of their purposes the first shop was called Chester's and at the far end there was Morris the picture framer.

The town's evening entertainments always seem to have been centred around the Marlborough Square area. The Engineer's Arms has always been a very popular pub, but the end of the building which is now a lounge was once called the Assembly

The Engineers Arms & Public Hall c1900

15

Rooms, and there they held auctions for almost anything and everything.

Bensons Night Spot has of course changed names many times over the years, but at the turn of the century it was a small brick building called the Public Hall. We had visits from travelling drama groups entertaining with such plays as "Maria Martin" (Murder in the Red Barn), "East Lynne", and "Face at the Window". I think it was 6d on the chairs and 3d in the gallery. When the building was taken over by Mr Johnson it became "The Electric". A detached house stood next to the building, which belonged to the manager.

Coalville once possessed its very own roller skating rink. It was a wooden structure built on a piece of ground next to the Liberal Club. However, it was not a successful venture and was pulled down to make way for a small theatre called "The Olympia". Here we had some very good acts, and the late Sandy Powell appeared at the beginning of his career. All went well until the silent screen became popular, when Mr Deeming took over the premises, turning it into a cinema known as the Regal, and now of course it is the Bingo Hall. How fashion dictates!

On the site of the Co-op there stood a row of cottages and at the end was a double fronted house with a small farm at the back named Stablefords. Their garden ran alongside our school playground.

As an inquisitive child, I once asked my mother how our streets got their names. She told me that Owen, Jackson and Margaret Streets were all named after a Dr Owen Jackson and his daughter Margaret. James and Gutteridge Streets were after James Gutteridge, a shopkeeper. Vaughan Street after Dr Vaughan, whom I remember. Berrisford Street was called after a builder of that name. I believe all these personalities had served on the local parish council.

I could go on reminiscing, but as always time is taking over. As we old ones step down, I hope that the new generation will help to keep Coalville still a place worth remembering. I trust these recollections will be of interest, and that reading them will be as enjoyable as writing them proved to be for me!

COALVILLE AS I REMEMBER IT -

K.M. Donaldson

I was two years old when the First World War broke out, so some of my early recollections are of Coalville in wartime. One of the earliest is of going to Coalville in my grandfather's pony and float to queue for the margarine ration at the Maypole store on the High Street. The Maypole was one of the early chain-store grocers. Margarine came in big blocks to the shops and then was cut into the required sizes by the assistants who wielded with great dexterity a pair of wooden butter pats. The wartime ration of margarine would, I suppose, have been very small, but later one would buy it in pounds and half pounds. The assistant would cut off about the right size from the great yellow block that stood on the counter. He would then shape it into a rectangular block with his butter pats, which put a striped pattern on the top surface. It was then slapped on to a piece of wrapping paper, weighed and the weight adjusted, and wrapped.

I lived with my parents in a house on what is now known as Porter's Corner in Hugglescote. Coalville to us was a world away. Most of our basic needs were obtained at the small shops in Hugglescote. Milk, bread and meat were delivered to the door. When we required something beyond this, then there would be an expedition to Coalville. And we walked. There was no question of buying new pots and pans, the old copper kettles and brass saucepans lasted a lifetime. Sheets and towels were only replaced when outworn, not when they went out of fashion, the flat irons never went wrong, so it was mainly a question of hats, shoes and material, for my mother was a thrifty lady and made most of our clothes. (Not until I was at the University did I ever have a bought dress skirt). The great delight of these trips to a small child was the chance to visit the Penny Bazaar, a sort of fore-runner to Woolworths. This was in Belvoir Road, a dark narrow slit of a shop, with the counter piled with whips and tops, and sawdust filled balls on elastic, and little balls of rainbow wool for French knitting. Snobs and marbles could be found in their season, and as the name of the shop implied, the price was one penny. The goods in the first Woolworths, which came to the town later, were priced at sixpence maximum.

I well remember the magic day when I was bought some lace-up boots. Till then they had been button-ups, but to have lace-up boots was to be on the brink of adult-hood! Brown's was the shop to get boots and shoes. Their shop was on the High Street, somewhere opposite the Midland station. It was small and dark, and presided over by a kind lady who took a great interest in ones feet. It was not difficult to make up one's mind which shoes to take. The choice was limited.

Market Place & High Street. 1900

For dress materials, and hats, and gloves, one went to Drewett's shop, first in Hugglescote where they had a shop opposite the end of Fairfield Road and later in the High Street in Coalville. Mr Drewett was a very stern gentleman, very much occupied with the work of the Adult School. He was careful to see that his lady customers were not extravagant in their purchases, and if he thought they were he did not hesitate to say so. On the High Street too was the one fish and game shop, Onions and White. Otherwise our fish was obtained from a man with a horse and little dray who periodically came trotting down from Ellistown shouting "Mack-rel, Fresh Mack-rel", and then one went out to the dray with a plate and chose one's mackerel. No refrigeration in those days!

Occasionally there was the great expedition to Leicester for shopping. We would go on the train from the Midland station, and as it was often the Christmas shopping we were doing, my memory is of the cold platforms and the waiting rooms with big coal fires. Often we stayed all day in Leicester and returned home in the cold and dark and walked back to Hugglescote with our parcels, along the icy paths. Sometimes we got off at Bardon Station and then there was a long walk down the dark lane.

The trains were quite important in our lives. Just above where we lived was Hugglescote station which we used a lot. Goods were delivered there for my father's Building Merchants business, wagon loads of slates from North Wales, roofing timber, cement and then these had to be offloaded onto a horse and cart and taken to our yard. Even during the first war there must have been some movement of goods as I have heard men say they remembered my mother helping to load slates that were frozen together. The train too was our route to the great wide world. I had an aunt who lived in Whitwick and we went there on the train, and we used that line too, to go and see my grandmother who lived in Coventry. That was Adventure, as we usually had to change at Shackerstone and Nuneaton. When I first went to Coalville Grammar School, the Junior Annexe was then in the house at Broom Leys which is now- Broom Leys Primary School. We went from Hugglescote station to Coalville East station at the bottom of Charnwood Street, and then walked round the cinder path at the back of Ellison's farm, or up Broom Leys Road, where I recall no houses on the right hand side and very few on the left. At some point in that time there was a rail strike and we had to walk to school and subsequently I never went to school by train again, which goes to show that strikes lose business! We also used that line to go to Loughborough where our dentist was. It was a jolly little railway train, with basket seats, the backs of which moved back and fore to face whichever way you wanted. Here and there was a place where the engine took on water, and there was the never failing excitement of watching the driver and the porter exchanging staffs, and hoping that one of them would drop it.

19

Sounds play a part in ones memories, too. I still hear the sound of the butter pats slapping the margarine, and I hear too the sound of men's feet tramping round the corner on their way to work, for in the pre-twenties men walked to the pits. Bicycles came later and after that special pit buses. One would hear the sound of tramping feet, a sort of dawn chorus, growing in an approaching crescendo in the cold dark of the morning, as they went for the early shift. There was one man who had a club foot who could not keep pace with the others, and he had to start earlier so his were the first steps to be heard. In the bicycle days and even more in the special bus era, the corner where we lived became very dangerous in the afternoons when the first shift was coming off. Of course, all the men were in their pit black, there were no pit baths then. Their bicycles had lamps which were run on carbide, and I remember a tub of this in my grandfather's shop. Another sound I recollect was the sound of the pit hooters. Each pit's hooter had a slightly different note, and one could tell the time by them. It was a grand sight, too, to be in Belvoir Road when the hooter went at Burgess's and all the work people came rushing out. There was the sound of the hand bell rung by the "okey" man, the forerunner of Jack's Ice Cream van with their musical chimes! I hear also the hiss of the naphthalene flares that lighted the market stalls in the dark winter evenings.

One of the most pleasing things to have seen in Coalville is the improvement in living standards and greater prosperity all round. Before the Second World War, the wealth of the town was centred on a few families, and the working people were generally speaking not at all well off. The property in Belvoir Road, and Highfields and Forest Road, on the Hugglescote side of the Grammar School was poor, with no amenities. Even our family had no running water from a tap until I was into my teens, no bathroom and no inside loo. For lighting, until I was three or four years into my secondary education, I worked by gas, oil or candle light. But now the housing in Coalville is well looked after, well improved. There has always been a great interest in horticulture, and one remembers the Hugglescote

Flower Show, and many gardens tended with loving care. I remember the greenhouse kept by old Mr Lander at Hugglescote Mill, which was full of the most exotic begonias, and a flourishing grape vine. There was a beautiful garden and lawn kept by Mr Edward Orton where now is the Orton Industrial Estate.

I should like to think I shall live long enough to see what changes come when the mines close and the nature of the town alters.

THE GOOD OLD DAYS? -
Mrs J. Grewcock

I was brought up with elderly grandparents. I was the eldest of 13 children but did not spend much time with my seven sisters and two brothers, because my grandparents needed help.

It provided me with a home and I obtained a job at a local factory to support myself, working from 7.30 a.m. to 5.00 p.m. each day at the factory and doing all the necessary housework in the evenings. I will describe the weekly routine.

On Monday evenings after work I did the weekly wash. First of all the copper had to be filled from the soft water well, which most houses had in those days. The soft water in the well was collected from the roof of the house, and was brought in by lifting out a bucketful on the end of a chain or rope and carrying this into the house. To heat the water, I used to collect all the burnable household rubbish e.g. coal slack, tea leaves, potato peelings, old leaves, rags and wood, and burn this under the old iron copper. It was a useful way of getting rid of all the old rubbish.

Tuesday evenings were spent in ironing and sewing all clothes needing ironing and doing needlework repairs, e.g. replacing buttons etc.

Wednesday evening was allocated to cleaning the three bedrooms in the house and the stairs. All the woodwork, which was usually dark brown or green had to be well polished to make it shine and this cleaning duty was extended to Thursday evening also.

21

On this evening, I cleaned all the brass and silver ware in the house. Most people had brass fire-irons and most of the cutlery was either silver or steel. Many brass ornaments were used to decorate the old fasioned fireplace and they also needed cleaning.

Then I cleaned the piano. Each key had to be cleaned once a week to stop the white ivory keys going brown. A large 'Wot-Not' was full of china ornaments, which used to collect dust from the coal fire, and these were washed weekly. We never had carpets on the floors, which were red tiled and had to be scrubbed on Monday nights with the soapy washing water.

On Friday night, after black-leading the fireplace, the red tiles would need scrubbing again and then the best pegged rug would be spread on the hearth for the weekend. These rugs were made from old clothes, cut into strips about 3 inches long and these were pegged through an old sugar bag, which was bought from the 'Co-op' for sixpence. This sugar bag was opened up at the seam, washed and then dried flat to make work easier on your fingers. Every piece of material had to be pushed through the sacking with a peg and a pattern was made up as you went along. Lots of families would sit through the long winter nights making these rugs which would last for ages. The rugs could be washed and used up all the scrap cloth materials produced by the family.

Saturday was the day for cleaning toilets and windows, shopping and bathing. Bath night was a real fun night. First we had to fill the copper, as on washday, and a good fire would be started to heat the oven and water tank. The old tin bath would be filled and we would bathe and wash our hair in carbolic soap. Vinegar was then used to rinse our hair, so that no soap was left, and it would shine beautifully when dry.

For supper on Saturday, we would have roast potatoes and mushy peas as a real treat before going to bed.

On Sunday we went to Church three times and then we were back to work on Monday again.

I never had time to sit and get bored, there was always a job to be done such as taking two dogs for a walk, helping to clean out the hen pen, feeding hens and collecting eggs. Helping to set potatoes with my grandfather was always fun, but it was better still to dig them up in the autumn and store them in a clamp for the winter. We always saved our own peas and beans for the following year by drying all the pods until brown and then threading the beans on a string to dry off.

Seasonal Activities

Autumn always brought lots of interesting things to do, such as gathering blackberries for jam making, elderberries for wine making, wheat gleaned from the field after harvest was also used for wine making and nettles were collected for nettle beer. Herbs collected from the fields were dried and stored to make herb tea to drink during the winter months.

Herbs in those days were always thought of as a medicine and people would set aside part of their garden for herbs for use in cooking. Root crops would be collected, cleaned and stored away in the back bedroom where the frost could not enter. Nothing was ever wasted and many things were home made. Lots of people made their own bread and cakes and by the time the dark nights came around we were making mince meat and plum puddings ready for Christmas.

The Christmas cake was always made before the end of November so that it would stand for a few weeks before icing and decoration. We would also spend hours peeling small onions and chopping red cabbage to make enough pickle to last through the next twelve months. Apples and pears were also stored and crab apple jelly.

After school, in early November, we would go out collecting dead leaves and old wood to make a bonfire, but I never had any fireworks. We did have lots of treacle toffee, or Black Ball, as it was called, which our parents made several days before. It was a real treat to eat.

Church and Sunday School

Church played a big part in my life at that time. There was always something going on. Every season would bring something different and, if you wanted to get your own Bible, you had to attend at least 48 times out of 52 in the year. If you repeated the same in the next year, you earned your Hymn and Prayer Book. Our Sunday School treat was held at Spring Hill Farm and we would walk there, play games and have tea before walking home. If you were lucky you were selected to go with the teacher to the Monastery.

The Monks would take us behind the scenes to watch them at their work, getting stones and materials to build the new Church. They would give us a drink of milk and some fruit to eat on our walk home.

Good Friday was always a day like Sunday. No one went to work but we all enjoyed our Hot Cross Buns and Easter Eggs.

School Days

Empire Day was a great day at our school when every girl was dressed in white and every boy was in grey and white. We all had a Union Jack flag and danced in the playground and sang to England, Ireland and Wales.

Armistice Day was another great day treated with respect in our school. We sang songs for all the Nations and the Hymn 'O Valiant Hearts' would be sung after the two minutes silence was observed by everyone.

Everyone in those days had a Red Poppy to wear, which cost 2d, but we seemed proud to wear one to remind us of the Great War. The day was a sad one for so many people, who had lost their fathers. I was lucky because my father was a prisoner in France and I was four years old when he came home. He was in poor health as a result and couldn't find any work, so he and my mother went up to live with one of my aunts in Barrow-in-Furness. My father got a job in the shipyard there.

I stayed behind with my grandparents and have remained here ever since. My parents ended up with a very large family of which ten of us are still alive, but, sad to say, my parents died quite early in life. They had a very hard struggle but always seemed happy. I always used to wonder how they could stay so loving towards each other and yet be so poor. Maybe the thoughts of the war and being parted for four years made them happy to be together again.

I remember one of my uncles coming home from the war with

one foot missing and his other leg off up to his knee. He was so happy to be home and alive. He used to sing in the choir before he went to the war and, when he came home after a lot of treatment in hospitals, he was given one of the invalid chairs supplied to wounded men. A local Catholic Priest called Father Degan used to come and take my uncle for a 'walk' as far as the Monastery and back. I was about 6 years old at the time and had many a ride on the foot rest of the chair sitting between my Uncle's artificial legs. I had many a cup of tea with Father Degan, who was a good man to the poor people of those days, getting shoes and clothes for the poor children and many adults as well.

Entertainment

He kept a few pet monkeys and a parrot as well as other foreign birds. Children were allowed to help him feed "his little zoo". He was a good organiser of social events to help ex-servicemen and their families, eventually opening a place for dancing and whist drives, which became very popular, particularly with the young people in the area.

The Salvation Army helped many people in those hard days and, for one penny, we could go to their building once a week to see a piece of film on a magic lantern, have a sing-song with the Band and then have something warm to drink. I used to have cocoa, but if you were lucky you could have soup, and at Christmas, we were given an apple and an orange to take home.

Every village would have its own wake, which was quite a big event. At the fair, families and friends would gather together to enjoy the weekend with lots of home made pies, cakes, home-made wine and always a piece of cooked ham if your family were lucky to have had a pig.

Each season and event led to the next throughout the year and everyone was busy preparing according to the tradition for the next event right up to the 1926 strike, which was a very long and hard struggle.

Playtime

We played a lot of games such as whip and top, snobs, marbles, hopscotch, shuttlecock and battledore, skipping, paper chase, leap frog and hide and seek. Most of us had a hoop, wood for girls and iron for the boys, and we used to run miles behind it around the streets. The street was our playground as there was not much traffic about at the time.

Bread, milk and coal were delivered by horse and cart and only the rich had a bicycle. I never saw a bus or car except on the main road to Leicester and they were few and far between. There were trains to Ashby and Burton but money was so scarce, if I wanted to go somewhere I went on foot most of the time.

There was always Bradgate Park and Coalville Park to enjoy and it was pleasant to listen to a good Band playing in the park after Church on a Sunday night.

Illness in my schooldays

Measles. Nearly everyone had it and we were put to bed until the spots had completely disappeared, being given hot soup and milk drinks.

Mumps. When I had this, I had my neck painted with Iodine and kept warm in bed.

We had a Typhoid scare while I was at school and we were sent home and given Friars Balsam on a lump of sugar. Sulphur powder was blown down my throat and I was given lots of Herb tea to drink. Smallpox came to Ibstock one year, but did not spread to Coalville.

I can't remember much about a Doctor until I had Rheumatic Fever. He was a coloured man and his name was Doctor De Souza (Desuzer?). He was very kind to me and used to call at night time and stay with us. My grandparents would make small bags as long as my arms and legs, fill them with common salt and put them in the oven to get really hot. They would then place them under each arm and leg until they were cool, continually replacing them night and day. The Doctor stayed with me many nights in the following weeks and gave me a small silver cross to hang around my neck and a copper bracelet to wear, one day on my right wrist and the next on my left.

The treatment seemed to go on for a long time and he told me stories about his home country and how poor the people were. I always feel I owe my life to that coloured man. I was 12 years old and after spending almost a whole year at home, I was very pleased to get back to school to join in everything once more.

Medicines and Remedies

For cuts - Zambuk For corns - Union Jack paste For rough skin - Snowfire cream

Goosegrease was saved after each goose was cooked, and was stored in a stone jar. It was rubbed on a person's chest to cure Bronchitis, Pneumonia, Whooping Cough.

Eucalyptus was used on sugar for sore throats and colds.

Camphorated Oil was used for earache. When there was a 'flu' epidemic, we all had a Block of Camphor sewn in a small linen bag hung around the neck until it melted away, helped people breathe more easily.

Brimstone and Treacle was taken to clear spots on the skin and ulcers in the mouth.

Epsom Salts were taken for upset stomach and constipation.

Linseed on Bread or Soap and Sugar was used as a poultice to clear all pus from boils and abscesses.

Methylated Spirits were used for all kinds of stiff joints and sprained muscles.

Starting to work

I left school at 14 at Easter, but had to wait until August to get my first job as a 'run-about' at Clutsom and Kemp. I started at 30 a.m. and worked until 12 noon with one hour for lunch and nished at 5.30 p.m. I had to clean and dust around the machinery taking all dirt to the boilerhouse for burning. At the nd of the week I received 8/-, but 1d was stopped from my wages for Leicester Royal Infirmary. Nobody minded this because it was of great importance to everyone and that is how that Hospital became the great place it is today.

After doing the cleaning jobs for about 6 months, I was put on a job threading buttons on to a tape for use on suspenders. We had to thread 144 for 1 1/2d and some weeks I earned 9/6d per week, out of which I received 9d pocket money. I spent 6d of this going to see a film on Saturday afternoon, 1d on either 2oz of mixed sweets, or 1lb of broken biscuits, which were made to last a week, and 2d was for the collection at Church. I used to take one or two broken biscuits a day to work because we never had tea breaks in those days. We could also take apples or pears from our own fruit trees, which nearly everyone had, or eat a piece of raw carrot or turnip or celery as a change.

One day, one of the older girls left and I was given her job on a Press, which used to fit a buckle on to a length of elastic web to make part of a suspender. I had to use both hands and both feet to operate the machine and earned 2 1/2d for 144 pairs. This was good pay, which made my wage go up to 16/11d most weeks, out of this I was given 2/6d pocket money. I used to save some of this for several months and go to Leicester to get a skirt (4/11d), a jumper (2/6d) or cardigan (3/6d) from Marks and Spencer's. Nothing cost more than 5/- in that store, and Woolworths sold everything less than 6d so that we could get some make-up and scent and feel very grown up to go on the firm's outing.

This outing was a day trip to Skegness. We started from Coalville Station at 7.30 a.m., breakfast being served on the outward journey and dinner on the way home at night. It was great to be waited upon by waiters dressed in their uniforms and get two really good meals. The firm was a good concern to work for. It was near my home and I did not have to pay travel fares, so I had no reason to leave the job, which lasted all my working life.

After two or three years in one room learning all the different kinds of machinery, I was given a charge-hand's position giving work out to other girls and collecting work in. I enjoyed every minute of it and gained a rise every year of 5/-, and by saving hard managed to buy myself a bicycle for seven pounds and 10s at the age of 19. Then I bought a tennis racquet for 10s so that I could play on the firm's courts once or twice a week.

Around this time Clutsom and Kemp's factory began to expand and new machinery was brought in and new ideas tried out. Everybody seemed happy at their work and if one person started to sing everybody would join in. Then jokes would pass around the rooms like wildfire and we all seemed to have time to enjoy helping each other if anybody was in difficulty. We had a Swear Box, a Weather Box and Christmas Gift Box into which you had to put 3d if you offended, by swearing or telling lies.

The years seemed to fly by and the really good years came when corsets and roll-ons came into fashion. We had orders coming in from all over Britain and small orders from abroad.

Further Thoughts

Mill Dam, Stablefords Pond. Swimming Gala once a year.

Three Horse Shoes Inn. Annual throwing of horse shoes. Miners from most of the mines used to get together in the summer evening and hold their tournaments, then have a supper of black puddings, peas and pigs trotters.

Half Way House Inn. Used to hold a wild beast show once a year. Most animals would be in tents all week and on a Sunday morning they would be paraded around Coalville Streets. That was the nearest people ever got to a circus. Then, as time went by, that same field became the greyhound track as it is today.

Co-op Treat. Once a year all the children from miles around would meet at the Marlborough Square bringing their own cup and following the bands which would play all the way to a field at Ravenstone. Each child would be given a bag containing a sandwich, cake and sweets, and a man named Mr Johnny Jennings used to dance most of the way back in the evening to the music of one of the bands. He was a man who always wanted to entertain people and was well known throughout Coalville.

Now on to a few more people who will be remembered for their part of Old Coalville:-

Mr Vessey's fish and chip van in the Breech Road. He gave a treat to children every Thursday night of a small bag of chips and scratchings which was enjoyed by many who were lucky enough to get one.

Mr Guy: He kept a furniture shop in Central Road. He used to repair wicker chairs and baskets and mended all kinds of antiques and upholstery. He used to like to talk to young people about his trade.

Mr Jones: He was a piano tuner. Although he was a blind man, people were fascinated at the way he went about his work. He depended on his hearing and nimble fingers, and was a very independent person and very interesting to talk to.

Mr Newberry: A lame and very frail little man. He used to walk around lighting the street lamps with a small type ladder on his shoulders.

Mr Fisher: He kept a chemist shop in Belvoir Road and was famous for his own cough mixture. He would also make his own perfume which always was a mixture containing oil of lavender and herbs.

Miss Kemp: A very old lady who owned a shop and bakehouse (end of Bridge Road into Belvoir Road). She sold all kinds of bread, cakes, yeast, flour and cheese and always had two very special cats sitting on her counter waiting to catch the mice which used to run from the bakehouse into the shop. Crickets could be heard all day and night. Then out she would come and sweep all the pavement around her shop with a large broom which was twice the size of herself. A very interesting old lady to talk to.

Mrs Green: Famous for her hot faggots and very tasty gravy.

Mr Willars: A very nice man to know, he was a gents hairdresser.

Mr Coulson: A well known photographer in Coalville before Mr Stacey took over.

Mr Fern: A nice little man, he had a shoe repairing business in his own front room and was very kind to people with little children and never charged them much at all.

Mrs Gutteridge: A nice lady who was a dressmaker. She also made baby clothes, nightdresses and lots of ladies underwear.

Mr Dicky Whitford: Only shop which had the three balls hanging outside (a pawn shop); became the foreign meat shop (Ingrams).

Lenton's Shop: Family shoe business.

Mr Vendy: A very friendly dentist.

Mr Chapman: A very friendly milkman.

Mr Plowman: Hardware dealer: Paraffin, carbide, tallow candles and china - everything from 'T. pots to P. pots'.

Mr Slater's Shop: Sold wheat, corn and meal for hens.

Mrs Aldridge: A fruit shop. She was a very interesting lady who used to sit all day making wreaths and bouquets. She would love to talk to anyone who was interested in flowers.

Mr Wallace: The Vicar of St. James' Church. A real friend to everyone.

Bazaar: A very interesting little place. You could buy a whip and top, shuttlecock and battledore, bombs and caps, pegs, clothes lines, games - one being Lotto which is called Bingo today. Shoe laces, matches, cotton etc. 2d, 4d, 6d was the most we paid for things until Woolworths opened their store and then out went the shop we used to love to walk around, especially on a dull and rainy day.

Hopkins: Fish and chip shop, Ashby Road, Coalville.

Sitdowns: Fruit shop. Lashmore the Jeweller: If you bought your wedding ring from them they always gave you a lovely gift to go with it.

Nurse Haywood: She was the district nurse for many years and had a word for anyone, rich or poor. She was a nice person to know and, if we saw her with her little black bag, we would sit and wait ages outside the place she was visiting until she came out and told us she had left either a little boy or girl. We believed her every time, thinking her bag contained the baby.

A Small Farmhouse: Was a building opposite Mason the Chemist. Every summer we used to see a little old gentleman. He would sit there smoking his clay pipe, and everyone would wave to him as they went about their shopping. We never knew his name, maybe someone will remember him.

Other forms of Entertainment

Grand old films at the Grand Theatre.

Cheap trips on the train at weekends for 2/6d return to Leicester, Burton or Birmingham.

Dancing at Father Degan's.

Sunday night Walk of the Town: Which was made up of 4 or 6 pals walking from the Marlborough Square up to the Station for maybe three hours, just for a chat, kiss or cuddle in Lashmore's opening. Sometimes there would be more than 100 people, 'young ones' of course, all walking behind one another enjoying themselves. We called it the 'Donkey Trot'.

MY VANISHED YOUTH -

Amy Hill

My earliest memory is of going to school "Christ Church Infants", now used as the Church Hall.

We had a teacher whose name was Miss Dean, Dolly Dean, and we all adored her. I remember in the hot summer days she would sneak us out of the end classroom, (the one which the babies occupied) and take us to have our lesson in the Church yard under the trees where it was cool and fresh. I was the one whom she sent into the classroom to see if it was time to come in, I felt so privileged. I could not tell the time, but I could tell her that the small hand was on the three and the large hand on the twelve.

How differently we all felt towards the Headmistress. She was "enthroned", or so it seemed, in the big room which housed three classes. She sat on a raised platform in the middle of the room, where she could see everyone. How fearsome she looked, her bulky figure clothed always in black, her hair parted in the middle and scraped back in a tight bun. Even her name was frightening, Miss Strickland. If she saw anyone talking or not paying attention her voice would boom out and we would all cringe in terror, though I can say honestly I never did see her punish anyone, her mere presence was enough to command instant obedience. She looked like Queen Victoria.

The Rev. Hoskins was the incumbent at Christ Church at the time, and he came into the school every day, mostly to take morning prayers. He was a very venerable gentleman. He had two unmarried daughters, who ran a Kindergarten school on London Road near the old cemetery.

My Aunty was the proprietor of the Fox and Goose Hotel. She was a widow. Her name was Mrs Butler. Her brother, who was my Uncle Ben, helped run the Hotel. I spent a lot of time there and used to run errands to the shops etc. During the first world war, my Aunty and helpers were packing parcels to send to the local boys at the front for Christmas and I was told to go to Harvey Morris' shop at the corner of Bakewell Street for some more long tin loaves as they had run short. I said "Do they have to be hollow like those?" pointing to some already on the table. Aunt Francis said "Oh no! for God's sake don't say anything about that." Apparently they were cutting out the middle of the loaves and putting in the loaf a bottle of whiskey, then packing it round and sticking the end back on. I suppose it was not allowed for the men to have whiskey in the trenches, but I can tell you that many local boys did. After the war I remember them coming in to see Aunty Francis, that is the ones who were lucky enough to come back, and presented her with a most beautiful solid silver tray which was inscribed. It is still in the possession of her grandson and greatly treasured.

I lived on London Road near the Coalville East railway bridge, with another aunt and uncle. I had lots of aunts and uncles and cousins, not to mention brothers and a sister. My uncle was away at the war and my aunty and I were at home together when the Zeppelin came over and dropped bombs on Loughborough. We got up and dressed, but it all seemed a bit pointless as there was nowhere we could go.

One of my early memories was going to the station in Hotel Street. Yes we had two stations in Coalville at that time! I went to meet my uncle who was coming home on leave from France. I would be about eight years old.

I can see him now. He wore a tunic style jacket and a peaked cap, and puttees on his legs and carried a kit bag. He said he'd arrived in England the previous day but had had to go to a centre, I think it was Folkestone, to be deloused. How horrified I was to think he had ever had lice and how little I knew at that time of the unspeakable deprivations they suffered.

Later on, when my uncle was reported missing, I realised how many homes were going through the misery we suffered. Fortunately he had been take to a field dressing station with mere shrapnel injuries, so we really were very lucky, but mostly the long lists of those missing were never to come home to their loved ones.

At one period during the first war Broom Leys was occupied by refugees from Belgium, as that country was completely overrun. I had some Belgian children to my house to play with me. We seemed to get on together fine in spite of the language barrier.

Later on in the war, Broom Leys was a convalescent home for the war wounded. It was a common sight to see them hobbling around the lanes on crutches in their bright blue flannel suits, with red collars.

These soldier boys gave a Concert at the Olympia Theatre which my aunties attended and said how much they had enjoyed it.

At the age of 14, I started to play the Violin. I took it very seriously and practised many hours each day. (How my aunt and uncle must have suffered).

After a year or so I joined the Coalville and District Orchestral Society, though it was not called that at the time. We used to practice in the Progressive Hall, which was at the back of the Liberal Club in Marlborough Square.

Coalville Philharmonic Orchestra at the Baths Hall. 1935

The Orchestra had between 30 and 40 members, who came from all walks of life. There were miners, engineers, factory workers, school teachers, a bank clerk, mining official, and a doctor's wife.

At the Baths Hall every year we gave a Celebrity Concert and engaged one or two professional musicians or artists. I enjoyed my years with the Orchestral Society and played with them for

14 years. Mr Jonathan Burton was the Conductor at the time I joined, and afterwards his brother conducted us. The Burton family was very well known in local music circles, as were the Benistons and Shaws. Several members of these families played in the Orchestra. Each Autumn, the members and Choir of the Ebenezer Chapel produced an Oratorio, and members of our Orchestra were asked to help.

Mr Frank Newman was the musical director and, although I believe his musical education was scanty, his enthusiasm was boundless, and by his sheer personality, he drew out the best from the singers and instrumentalists alike. He bullied and cajoled, he castigated and flattered, but in the end he always achieved the excellence he was seeking.

These musical productions were eagerly anticipated by the public and were always sold out long before the date. Mr Newman was later to be appointed the Musical Director for the Coalville Amateur Operatic Society, where I was asked with other members of our Orchestral Society to play. We all had many happy years together and it took another World War to break it all up.

CHILDHOOD MEMORIES OF COALVILLE IN EARLY 1900 -
Mrs E.M. Hill

I was born in Shepshed on March 1st 1899, coming to Coalville with my parents at the age of three, and have now lived here for 81 years. My father came to work at the Co-operative Bakery Department as a Bread Checker and was there for 40 odd years. The bakehouse was then in Owen Street, where the back of the Co-op shops are now. At the side of the bakehouse was the stoke-hole for the ovens, where you could often hear the crickets chirping. Next to that stood one house and a bit of waste ground, where now stands part of the Co-op Trendsetter.

My early schooldays were varied, as it was difficult to find me a place. I first started at an infants school held in the rooms at the back of Marlborough Square Chapel, and, when I had to go to a higher class, I was moved to another school at the back of the old Baptist Chapel, which stood at the corner leading to Hermitage Road, but is no longer there now. Things were very primitive and gruesome there for children. Down the small yard were one or two earth lavatories surrounded by graves and headstones. Our playground was across the road on a rough piece of ground where now stands a modern garage, and nearby was Nelson's Warehouse, a vast difference to today's schools. However, during this time, Bridge Road School was built and, when the others closed, we moved in. It was like moving to a palace from where we had just left, and of course, my schooldays ended there at the age of 14.

Before the houses and Forest Road Garage across the road from the Fox and Goose were built, the ground was used for some sort of races and people came from all over the place. I well remember sitting in my Grandparent's bay window in London Road watching the crowds wending their way to the station for home after a visit to the Fox and Goose first! The men and women all used to link arms stretching right across the road, singing and dancing merrily along with no traffic problems, as the traffic was nearly all horse-drawn in those days.

Another of my memories is located where now stands the Bingo Hall in Jackson Street. It was waste ground and periodically a travelling show used to come with a most magnificent front, all gilt and moving figures and a lovely sounding organ. All the figures moved to the rhythm of the music, which was a delight to me to hear and see. This would be about 1906, as my sister was then a baby, being 9 years my junior and, at that time, they put on a baby show and friends tried to persuade my parents to enter her, but to no avail. I remember one of the prizewinners was the baby of a Mr King, who was a well known chimney sweep, who the older people of Coalville will remember no doubt. Then the Olympia was built there and was used as a cinema, boxing booth and at one time a skating rink, where I used to enjoy watching the skaters. Now of course, it is a bingo hall.

Another special occasion to me was the flower show, which they used to hold on the Halfway House Field and engage a young lady, by the name of Dolly Shepherd, who used to go up in a balloon. It was quite exciting to stand and watch them blow it up and then take off. Then someone would drive off the field into the country in a pony and trap, always the tub style trap. I can see it now. They would follow the balloon, and try and locate where it was going to come down, and pick the young lady up. This was one of the main attractions that day. This field was also used as the assembly ground for the Co-op treat at one time, when each child was issued with a bag of food, a bar of chocolate, and a mug of tea. Later it was transferred to a field down Ashby Road, when we used to parade down there, led by several bands. There would be brandy snap stalls and several amusements on the field. All these special occasions meant so much to us in those days.

Flower show parade passing the 'Halfway House'

I also think back to when the present Broomleys School was the home of the Mansfield family. Mr Horace Mansfield, J.P., owned the Whitwick brickyard and my late mother's uncle, Mr Walter Brownlow, was Manager. In our Church at Marlborough Square Methodist is a plaque in memory of Mr Mansfield's wife. After the Mansfields had gone, the building was used as a refuge for a number of French and Belgian refugees during the first world war, and my parents used to invite some of them at weekends for meals. Then it finally became a convalescent hospital for our wounded soldiers. It was quite the usual thing to see them walking about in their light blue hospital suits and khaki hats, some on crutches, some with arms in slings, but they always seemed in good spirits. So over the years the building has done some good service, and still is doing with the school.

Another incident that comes to mind was the big fire at Burgess's elastic factory on Belvoir Road and, about the same week, was the Co-op Hot Cross bun scare when a Belgian refugee working there got hold of the wrong oil for cooking by mistake. The poor chap was in a terrible state when he knew, as all who had eaten them before the warning went out were falling ill. Everything seemed to be happening all at once.

We had no Leisure Centres etc. in our younger days as now, but found the enjoyment ourselves on the occasions mentioned in my memoirs. Another old landmark was the old farmhouse that stood at the corner of James Street where the car park is now. The owner was James Gutteridge, hence James Street and Gutteridge Street. At one time the Brotherhood family lived there, and, as a child, I used to play in the farmyard with their children. After the Brotherhoods, it was occupied by the Browns. Before the present Salvation Army hall was built, I remember them having a wooden building on that same ground as the farm was, but it came right up to the houses in James Street.

I also remember when Coalville used a hand cart to take round with the fire appliances and it was housed in a wooden shed at the Council yard up Highfields. There was a box at the side of the shed with a glass front which had to be broken to sound the fire bell and the firemen would come and run with the truck as fast as they could, but if it was a big fire, or a long distance, help would come from elsewhere.

Now I am left with these memories of my childhood days that stand out most in my mind, some happy, some sad, thinking of loved ones we had then and have now passed on, but truly thankful for having had good caring parents.

MEMORIES OF JOHN ROWLANDS HILL -

Mr J.R. Hill

The improvement of Mantle Lane in 1911. The old Mantle Lane went over a railway crossing to get to Thornborough and New Swannington. There was a brickyard on the right side of the road.

Wagons had to cross the road to get to this brickyard and when the brickyard finished, it was used to store 600 5" guns which were going to Russia. The new Mantle Lane crossed a field at the side of Stableford's Wagon Works. When the new road was taken under the railway line, the dirt extracted was tipped on the left hand side of old Mantle Lane where the old Wolsey factory, the power station and old Co-op Bakery stood later.

A cattle market was held at the side of the Red House on Tuesdays where, later, the old covered market was held. The Red House belonged to Mr Tyler. Another cattle market was held at Margaret Street. There was a Fair Ground on Market Street.

At the centre of Coalville there was a lamp and four wooden posts, where the Salvation Army played three times a week.

I remember the Post Office being built, also the Coalville Bus Garage. This was built, in 1914 by Coleman Bros, next to the Post Office on Ashby Road, which was originally Long Lane that ran from Hoo Ash to the Stone Cottages at Bardon.

On Good Friday 1917, Burgess's factory caught fire. Five engines, drawn by horses, came from Leicester and Ashby, since there was only a hand cart engine at Coalville.

The two main events of the year were the English Cup Final and Co-op Treat.

Two trains used to run from Coalville Station to the Final. Every pub used to have a sweep, and put so much money away for that day. The return price was 12/6d, and I used to run the sweep from the Waggon and Horses.

The Treat was attended by children in hordes from all the districts around. There were six bands which led the children in a parade from Coalville, to a field on Ravenstone Road. All had to take a mug with them for tea, and they were given a bag of food. This was a great day.

Improvement of the Shopping Centre, Precinct Car Park and Market Hall

There was a football field owned by Mr Evans where the Precinct is today. I used to play football there. There was a very deep clay hole where the car park is now, and I knew a man who was drowned in a pond in the bottom. Mr Watters' flour mill was where the Market Hall now stands.

Coalville Flower Show was a big event in the year, and besides the show, there were races for the children, and trotting ponies with gigs. Mr Henson, Mr King, Mr Fry, Mr Burton, Mr Moore and Mr Parker used to take part in the races.

For a special event of the day, Captain Gordon and Dolly Shepherd went up in a balloon to about 600ft, then Dolly would jump out and parachute down to earth.

There were Silver Cups given by Mr E. Horton, Mr Coleman and Mr Glover, and my father was a showman and won four cups. A big firework display closed the show.

I look back at my childhood when you could get a 5lb weekend joint of beef for 2/6d, which we took to the Co-op Bakery, and they used to cook it for 6d. Woodbine cigarettes were 5 for 1d and others were 10 for 3d. A hair cut cost 3d.

Coalville has seen many changes. The Olympia was built in

Coalville Public Hall. 1910

the early 1900's as a skating rink. This didn't last long, as it did not pay, and they changed it to stage plays, then to films, and finally now, as a Bingo Casino.

There were two long army huts where the Drill Hall now stands, where we used to do army training.

A Y.M.C.A. stood in Hotel Street, where a hairdressing salon now is, and there was a pot works where the Dole Building now stands.

Next to the Engineers Arms was the Public Hall. They used to have puppet shows there, until it changed to the Electric Theatre for silent films. It then changed to the Grand Ballroom, then Tiffany's and now Bensons.

COALVILLE AS I REMEMBER IT -
Mr W.J.E. Hill

Coalville as I remember it, seemed a poor, but a very cheerful place, with a smile and friendly word, even to a stranger.

My earliest recollections are of the tradesmen that came to our doors by horse and cart, or trap. The coalman, with huge lumps of coal on the dray, and the scales at the rear. The butcher; the milkman who came to the back door with his bucket to measure out the milk into your basin or jug. The man shouting "trap rabbit"; the baker blowing his whistle at the bottom of our entry, and, one Easter, I remember one lady when she asked "when are yo coming again?", asking for twenty four loaves, to which he said to the boy with him "unship the hoss".

I remember the miners' cottages along the Ashby Road, two up, and two down, with earth closets at the bottom of their gardens. Several families had in the teens of children. Most had no shoes, and their clothes were tattered and torn. I remember the 'knocker up' early in the morning, the lamp lighter with his long pole, putting the street lights out at 10 o'clock. The urinal that stood on the crown of the road near the Memorial Clock Tower. This was built by a local firm, and Bruce Dennis and his son laid the bricks.

I remember the local Flower and Vegetable shows, with all the fun of the fair, and the local bands giving a performance on the

41

Park. The churches and chapels were always full, and the concerts and artists were of top quality.

The steam trains had a smell of their own, and on more than one occasion I have counted the waggons on the two beer trains that passed through from Burton-on-Trent each night. Stablefords waggon works had a club down Mantle Lane and the large clay hole pond was where swimming galas were held. The diving board seemed to me as a child to be a terrific height. Fishing also took place. Unfortunately many a life has been lost in that pond and not all by accident. My father won a life saving certificate here.

I remember the two Leicester newspapers on a Saturday night, trying to see who would be first with the sports results. In those days it usually was the Mail.

The Coalville Charity Cup Final on Easter Tuesday, at the 'Waggon and Horses' ground always attracted a large crowd. Some 'pro' sides today would like a crowd like that turned out on that day.

We all adjusted our time pieces when the pit buzzer blew at the various times, and some of us can remember what the long blast that blew at the Whitwick Colliery that fatal day meant. The Co-op treat was a yearly event enjoyed by most, and a ride on the hay cart a couple of weeks before the event on the field where it was held seemed a treat in itself. As I finish I dare say many more memories will come back to me, but I trust these few will be a contribution.

COALVILLE AS I REMEMBER IT -
Mrs Evelyn E.G. Holland (nee Edwards)

I sit and reminisce at times about the things my mother and father used to do and tell me years ago. My father, whose name was Bill Edwards, and who would have been, if he was alive today, 86 in July, used to work the "Old Incline" at Swannington as a Fitters Mate alongside a Mr Robinson from Highfields. I can remember along with my sister Edie, going down. Walking from Queen Street, Coalville, along Thornborough Road, and over the stile, down to the Incline, which in our Summer Holidays from school was beautiful. Trees bending over, quiet, and so still down there, with no rush whatsoever in the air, everything was peaceful. We used to watch our Father let all the waggons go down hill right to the gate near to the outlet where the "Fountain Inn" stands in Swannington. My father also used to work behind the stage at the old 'Olympia', where the Bingo Hall now stands. He used to operate the scenery at the back alongside my mother's brother, Mr Horace Bott. As a teenager, I used to go backstage with my mother, who used to do all the washing for the artists, and stiffen white collars for the gents (and I say stiffen). They were as white as drifting snow. Alas, I threw the photos away when my mother died two years ago.

The 'Olympia'. 1912

Also, my mother, who was then called Edie Botts, from the age of 19 worked for 9 1/2 years, at the Conservative Club near the Railway Crossing. That would be about 1914. I have sent along two brass trays which the waiters used to use at that time of day, which were from the Conservative Club. My mother would have been 88 this May if she would have lived. She also told me about the butter she used to pat, pat, pat together at the old Maypole Stores in, is it Hotel Street or, High Street?

These little things are Coalville, and all it stands for. My Uncle's Leicestershire Regiment Monument is in Coalville Cemetery, on

43

the left side going in, near the wall, Pte Martin 1915. My parents told me he was the first soldier to be brought back to Coalville, and to be buried there. My mother said one could not move down London Road for people that day.

I wish I could say more, but my thoughts linger, and I think about all those little items I was told about and some of which I saw.

A CHILD OF COALVILLE -
Mrs G. Knight

I was born in 1923 in Gutteridge Street, Coalville, the youngest of four children. Looking back it seemed a lovely safe life, and certainly we were never bored. There always seemed so much to do. Of course, there were very few cars, so we could play whip and top, hide and seek etc. in complete safety.

One of the highlights for us was when the fair came. It was nearly always held in Mr Ward's field, against the old allotment fields, and I can remember lying in bed and seeing "Peg Leg" jumping from a high platform into a large tub which someone used to set on fire. Everyone used to wait with bated breath to see if "Peg Leg" crawled out all right, and I think he always did.

The sight and smell of the roundabouts was unforgettable. The huge traction engine used to throb and shudder until midnight when it was switched off, and everything was quiet, and we children could settle off to sleep. Our dad used to take us to the fair. At the entrance were stalls selling birds on long sticks and, if you twirled them round they made a lovely whistling noise. There were brandy snaps, "stick a rock" and little ginger biscuits sold, as it seemed to us, by real gypsies. We were told to behave ourselves or they would steal us, and we would be lost forever.

Dad always won a coconut at the shies. He knew just where to aim for because he used to make the shies at Wootton Bros. which was on the site of the present Key Markets.

Once or twice a week David Smith used to visit the street selling lovely yellow home-made icecream from his pony cart Of course, in those days "Tupperware" was unheard of, we all used to troop out with cups and basins, and he used to fill them up to the top for 6d. Then we would sit on the kerb eating it with a spoon. How lovely it was!

On Pancake Day we went along to Mr West's shop, or Bishop's against the Belvoir Road school, to buy skipping ropes, and shuttlecocks and battledores. Miss Saunders, our headmistress, always gave us a half a day holiday. It was a true "Coronation Street" even down to the little corner shop which sold everything.

One of the things we dreaded most was the day Ward's the butchers killed the pigs; the poor creatures seemed to be squealing all day, and we hated it. The Co-op bread vans used to be pulled by big beautiful horses, and often they would be led to stables somewhere at the bottom of Owen Street, promptly followed by men with shovels and buckets; to help the roses grow I expect.

Most of my playmates, including our family, were "Chapel". Our family favoured the Methodist Chapel in Marlborough Square, where my mother was a choir member for many years. We children had to go to Sunday school morning and afternoon. The highlight of our year was "the Sermons". We would be practising all the hymns for weeks, and the great day always seemed to dawn bright and sunny. Relatives from far and wide, young and old, came for this great occasion.

Off we went in our new frocks, with a warning from mother to pick our frocks up before we sat down, in case the specially built platform was dirty. The march was always my favourite. We sang with the band at the tops of our voices, making so much noise it didn't matter if we were out of tune.

I suppose a great many people of my generation will remember the Exchange Buildings.

Over what is now the Electract shop in Belvoir Road, there used to be a large room, which every now and then was visited by a company of actors. Such plays as "Love on the Dole" and "Maria Martin" or "Murder in the Red Barn" were performed, and pantomimes at Christmas. What excitement! We were too young to understand all that went on, but we sat through everything. One day a notice was nailed on the door announcing a "Yo-Yo" competition. The winner would receive a white rabbit. I had never had a rabbit; dozens of cats and dogs, but never a rabbit! I must have had plenty of nerve, but I entered and to my delight won. Imagine my disgust when an "old fairy", she must have been at least fifty, gave me a pile of sticky toffee, saying they couldn't get a rabbit.

I went home crying. My father took me back demanding my prize, but alas, I never got my rabbit.

At the chapel, our annual Sunday school outing was usually in the form of a visit to 'Spring Hill Farm'. The very name is beautiful. It always seemed to be a scorching day. We scholars had tea, consisting of bread and butter, plain slab cake, fruit cake and mugs of tea, in a long room at the farm. Games were held on a flat piece of field behind the farm, and afterwards we were allowed to climb the rocks. I felt as if I had been to the end of the earth. When our parents took us, we boarded a bus for Whitwick Market Place, and then had a long long walk up Leicester Road. If mother took us, after we had had our picnic, we used to pick the bilberries. These we put in ordinary paper bags and the trouble they caused! The juice would run over our fingers and clothes, but it would all be worth it when a bilberry pie would be put in front of us at dinner. All gone now, even the farm. I remember too the awe we used to feel, if we caught sight of the monks from the monastery working in the fields.

Generally, we walked home along Abbey Road by the 'Forest Rock Hotel', where we children sat outside whilst dad fetched us lemonade, and he and mum had a well deserved drink of beer.

Sometimes when we were older, dad would take us as far as 'The Bull's Head' pub, in those days it was a farm, and we children would have a glass of milk, often warm, straight from the cow. Frowned on today, but then it tasted like milk, thick and foamy and yellow.

One of the highlights of the year was the "Co-op Treat". I think it was held in August, either the Saturday or the Monday. All the children of Co-op members were asked to assemble in Marlborough Square. What an attractive square it was, lined with trees, no cars, a grand meeting place. Children came from all the surrounding villages and there would be hundreds of children

46

all of us carrying cups or mugs, with Brass Bands to lead us. Snibston, Whitwick and Desford bands would strike up, and we could have marched for ever, or so we thought, because for little legs it seemed a very long way from Marlborough Square to the field at Ravenstone turn, which is along Ashby Road. Our parents used to say they would be in a certain spot, and we must remember to look for them and not forget to wave.

The Co-op Treat mustering in Marlborough Square. 1900

Excitement grew as we neared the field, and all over the field were high mounds of bags, by this time looking decidedly greasy. We fell upon them as if we were starved, the rough boys diving in first. In this magic bag were sandwiches, rolls, the eternal plain and fruit slab cake and a bar of Co-op chocolate, usually a melted lump by now. Then we had to take our cups to large urns to get our tea. I never really liked it but had to go. Later in the evening, when the big fair started up, we would meet our mum and dad at a pre-arranged place, and once again sampled the delights of flying horses, dodgems, chair-planes etc. How young we seemed for our age, I cannot imagine today's children doing this.

Everyone, or so it seemed to me, went to the Hugglescote Flower Show held on a field in Crescent Road.

Huge tents were erected for showing flowers, vegetables, fruit and handicrafts, and the standard was very high indeed, I remember how proud we all were when my eldest sister won a prize with the picture she had worked in beautiful silks.

The highlight of the day for the adults was the cycle racing, I believe that entries came from many miles around.

Christmas time was a great occasion in our family. I know that our family and my friends had very simple toys, certainly nothing like the grand toys children of today have, and certainly not so many.

One of the memories of my childhood is going to bed with my sisters on Christmas Eve. Later on, we would hear the choirs from the chapels come round singing carols, and in the distance the bands. Nothing I have heard today sounded sweeter, indeed, we knew then it really was Christmas.

As I have said previously, my mother was a member of the choir. She had a good voice, contralto, and once every year the Ebenezer Chapel on Ashby Road would perform one of the great oratorios, Handel's Messiah, Elijah, Jephtha etc. As I remember, a lot of choir members from other chapels would attend, under the baton of Mr Frank Newman. He was a marvellous conductor and the singing was of a very high standard.

My mother and my friend's mother always went on a Tuesday evening to the choir practice and we had to go too. To persuade us to go we were given enough money to buy sweets, to keep us quiet no doubt. Anyone remember the A.I. sweet shop and Joblings? Real sweet shops! Anyway, it took us about half an hour deciding on a quarter of sweets, and then we would sit for a couple of hours listening to glorious singing, and young as we were, we loved it. Handel's Messiah was performed in December at the Marlborough Square Chapel. People, it seemed to me, loved these evenings, and I often wonder why they are just memories, the togetherness seems to have disappeared. At our chapel there used to be a concert once a month, and I remember that I joined the Young Fellowship group. Those in charge put on a play called "Tiaras and Tangles", I was a dreadful actress, but for some reason they chose me for the "lady", with Norman Bird playing the part of the "lord". Things went from bad to worse this

48

particular evening, and in the last act I had to sweep out of the french windows in a temper. I swept all right, but someone had forgotten to put the step there. As I fell I clutched the scenery taking the entire wall. End of acting career! Norman Bird went on to become a famous screen and television star. I wonder if he remembers one of his first roles! We were both about fifteen years old. I might add that the applause was deafening.

At the Belvoir Road Chapel a group of ladies formed "The Young Leaguers" which was really for girls between the ages of about five to fourteen. Somewhere before I think I have said that we joined anything that was going, so we all went hoping that we would be lucky. Of course television was unheard of, and the concerts and plays were really outlets for all our high spirits. My guess is that plenty of middle aged ladies remember dancing as "woodland fairies", Chinese girls, etc. and in those days people really did turn out to support and applaud our efforts.

Then there was the "Monkey Trot". From the railway station crossing on High Street, to "Olivers" crossing on Belvoir Road every Saturday and Sunday night, hundreds of teenagers paraded. The lads with hair slicked down, the girls with kiss curls, all trying to catch someone's eye. Our parents threatened us if ever we went, but it was the height of ambition to be old enough to join in these weekend capers.

Behind my friend's house in Gutteridge Street was the old farm, pulled down now to make another car park. Many are the hours we have sat on the garden wall looking at the animals. Rumour had it that there were dungeons underneath the farm building and that it was haunted. We used to gaze hopefully when it was getting dusk, hoping to catch a glimpse of the ghost. Some bolder ones said that they had seen it, and we knew better than to doubt them.

"The Grand" in Belvoir Road also played a big part in our lives. Every Saturday afternoon we could see the films for 2d. Part of the entertainment was to queue. A good hour before the doors were opened we would all be there. It was fraught with danger. Woe betide anyone who tried to push in. Rival gangs of boys from the streets around would take charge. Fights and scuffles

The 'Grand'. Early 1970s

galore, they looked like the gang from the "Just William" books.

The noise inside the cinema was terrible, and the poor usherettes would run up and down shining a torch on fighting children. Everywhere there would be orange peel and apple cores flying about, and if you were silly enough to stand up, you soon had a good smack on the head.

In my opinion the heart went out of Coalville when the lovely higgledy piggledy market was pulled down. Friday was market day then, as now, but then the town used to come to life. What characters too! I'm sure many people will remember the "Orange King". My mother used to meet me out of school in the afternoon and we would go to the market, as later in the day the stall holders used to sell their goods very cheap. If it was cold she then took me along to the railway station waiting room, and we used to warm ourselves in front of the roaring coal fire.

One of my memories must include the grocery department of the Co-op store in Marlborough Square.

It was a delight to go to the "bacon side" and watch mother choose her bacon from huge sides of bacon all hanging up. You could have it sliced there and then as thick or thin as you wanted it. Best of all was to watch the money put into little boxes overhead, and then watch it bobble along on wires to the cashier, wait a while, then watch it come back with change and cheque, to be unscrewed by the assistant.

My memories of the times during the war would fill a book, so I will only mention one or two.

I worked in the offices of No.10 factory in Owen Street, which was a munition factory from Birmingham making Oleo legs for the Spitfire. The days were long and tiring, but one afternoon there was great excitement. We were all told to leave everything at once and go to the Grange fields. A huge land mine had been discovered in the farm yard next to the factory. Until it was made safe we spent a lovely two hours in the fresh air. My other memory is sad. Two of our playmates from our portion of Gutteridge Street were called up in the services. They never came back. Their names are inscribed on the war memorial.

These then are a few of my memories of Coalville when I was a child. All very ordinary, but I look back at them with real affection.

The 'Snibstone New Inn' c1910

EARLY DAYS OF WOLSEY LTD. -
Mrs Gladys Merrivale (nee Smith)

No doubt there are still persons in Coalville who will remember, that where Grieves Ltd. factory is situated today in Baker Street, before the 1920's, part of this was occupied by R. Walker and Sons Ltd., Hosiery Manufacturer, later known as Wolsey Ltd. This was a branch factory whose Head Office was King Street, Leicester.

The working hours in the beginning were 6.00 a.m. to 5.30 p.m. with a break for breakfast and lunch.

Wolsey Staff. c1930s

In 1930 the Bedean System, an American System, was brought to the Coalville factory. This was a time and motion system and, after a week or two, it was objected to, and a Sit-in Strike was started. After one week, the employees were given written notice to leave their employment. The strike then spread to the Leicester factories. A few at Coalville worked, which brought pickets here from Leicester, and several times the police were needed to see the workers away home safely. The strike lasted 5-6 weeks. It was eventually found that this new system was not workable in this kind of industry owing to the seasonable changes in patterns.

n the late 1920's, tennis courts and bowling greens were laid in front of the factory. Tennis, hockey and bowling teams were formed, and all the teams did quite well. The Bowls team won the Gracedieu Cup, which is still played for today, and the Hockey team won the Inter-Factory Wolsey Cup.

The Wolsey Sports and Welfare Club was formed in the 1920's, possibly the fore-runner of all Sports Clubs in the district. Membership fees were as follows:

Men 4d per week, Women 3d per week Boys under 18 years 2d per week Girls under 18 years 1 1/2d per week

During sickness, benefits were paid out as follows:

men - 20/- per week for 4 weeks 10/- per week for 4 weeks 5/- per week for 12 weeks women - 10/- per week for 4 weeks 7/6 per week for 4 weeks 5/- per week for 12 weeks

Boys and girls received half the adult rates.

LETTER FROM ROBERT STEPHENSON TO HIS FATHER SHORTLY AFTER MOVING TO ALTON GRANGE, NOVEMBER 7TH 1830. -
David Ramsey

I, David Ramsey, have become Robert Stephenson. The observations made in the letter are those Robert would have been able to make during November, 1830, not long after his move to Alton Grange.

Dear Father,

At last I am able to report that I am established at Alton Grange and that the last chest, portmanteau and valise liberated of their contents, are now in storage.

The Leicester and Swannington Railway has taken much of my time and the Glenfield Tunnel in particular. My new designs for the tunnel entrances have been well received and my resolve to use Mountsorrel granite has gained full approval.

William Martin, Lord Stamford's Land Agent, has sent word that his efforts to attract further shareholders to the L & S alliance have been largely unrewarded locally and that he requests that word of the suitability, propriety, advantages and opportunism of

53

the venture be broadcast widely in the Liverpool and Manchester areas. I replied that my father was already working tirelessly to that effect!

You will remember that, in my last letter, I wrote of how my interest in the proposed London and Birmingham Railway would necessitate my acquiring a larger stable of horses? Well, after the L & S meeting, Lord Stamford informed me that he has two hunters, which are particularly sure footed and sound of wind, for sale at Groby, and knowing that gentleman's eye for quality, I feel I shall next report confirmation of purchase.

The weather here is damp and raw, not at all complimentary to my chest, but in spite of this debilitation, I have again made a long examination of the land you purchased to the north of the Ashby Turnpike.

Whilst surface scrapes in the past have exposed small amounts of coal in this area, may I command your attention to the fields three quarters of a mile further along the Turnpike towards Ashby, for I think speculation here may reward us even more handsomely.

I had last week noticed the drovers' beasts gathered in this area and, on later inspection of the fields exteriority, found in one particular scrape of a seam of coal close to two and a half cubits rising to the surface! As I mentioned beforehand Lord Stamford and I have horse business to attend to in three days time, so I shall enquire into the possibilities of land purchase at the same time; without being too specific.

The Turnpike from Leicester to Ashby is now even worse to travel. Stenson's Long Lane coal is being increasingly hampered by the rutted state of the Turnpike surface, additional perfunctory weighing machines, placed at even shorter distances than before, and those in charge of the toll gates take great delight in stopping hauliers and measuring the width of waggon wheels most frequently. This causes great pertubation of mind to mine owners and carters alike.

Stenson and others have of course taken great steps to improve the Turnpike twixt Long Lane and Ashby, financed from their own pockets, but from a practical engineer's view, I note that the lack of good base metalling means improvements are soon lost in its muddy depths and the name of Ditching Lane well chosen!

Stenson's miners are housed close to the pits in small houses owned by him. Two small rooms on the ground floor with garret rooms, open to the roof above. Deal planks laid over the joists suffice as both floor and ceiling, dividing the two levels.

They are happy families, not overworked at ten hours per day, resting on the sabbath, but being few in number, the mining men for our own ventures must surely be attracted from the northern coalfields and I would welcome your thoughts on this matter father.

Your obedient son,
Robert.

NOSTALGIA -
J.E. Reece

It is only by a fluke that I would have known about the competition, having travelled to Coalville on a wet Wednesday evening with my sister to the performance of "Calamity Jane" and calling in for the cup that cheers, I saw a poster and said to my sister "I must enter for that". Friends of ours are in the Orchestra with the show and very good it was too!
So here goes:-

I lived in Bardon for ten years, from 1942 - 1952, with my family, and regretfully, mother, father and brother are deceased, and there is just my sister and I of the original family.

My life at that time consisted of journeying to work each day, to which I cycled every morning at 7.15 a.m., Winter and Summer. I recall in the Spring and Summer, the sun and the morning air, and my joy of this and the exercise, both of which I have always loved. I walked on Bardon Hill and cycled to the St. Bernard Monastery often on a Sunday afternoon and enjoyed the peace of the Church there. Incidentally, at that time, there was no shop, and it was not at all commercial, but I visited it recently, and it still remains charming and peaceful.

I also, with laughter, recall the "Parade" (Sunday evenings) which all the young, ordinary, people did. There was little artificial entertainment in those days. The equivalent I experienced later was the "Promenade", during many lovely evenings spent in warm Italian cities.

I remember most of all the walking. To walk to Bardon from Coalville each evening from whatever activity you did was regarded as normal - not so much for us the "four wheeled chariot" of the modern child. Also, we thought nothing of cycling to Swadlincote to the Dances there on a Saturday, and to cycle back again full of the music and our memories of being asked to dance, by a handsome stranger whom we had talked to during this activity. Very difficult to make an acquaintance like that today, a somewhat difficult task now. How do the modern kids communicate and make their social contacts?

The "social" life of Coalville at that period centred very much on the "Baths". All dances and plays took place there and very enjoyable they were too. I recall a very interesting lecture on Gandhi - now very much in vogue and topical since Sir Richard Attenborough's film.

The 'Fox & Goose Hotel'. c1910

The good old 'Fox and Goose' at that time was always full, packed with the local characters, people who talked to one

56

another, not always glued to the television.

I have lived in the Leicester area now for many years. When you shop in the City you are rarely greeted by someone you know, but then, if you went "Up-Coalville", there was always a cheery greeting from someone, mostly "Ay-up" - "Ow are yer?" ...

The town is not architecturally thrilling to say the least. It always appears somewhat dark and satanic, but nevertheless aptly named as it is, of course, Coaltown! Sadly, the town is facing a lot of trouble industrially, let us hope that modern technology will provide more scope, some enterprising person maybe, what about video manufacture? ...

I have, since my days with you, travelled the world, well almost, my trips consist of France, Germany, Italy, Greece, Sardinia, Malta, Sicily, Rhodes, Cyprus, Morocco, America, The Bahamas, Canada, Spain, Ibiza, Mallorca, Menorca, Ireland, Rumania, Portugal, Yugoslavia, Belgium, Norway, Russia, Egypt and Israel -No I am not trying to show off just to say I still remember the past also.

Every Christmas, I am fortunate to visit the town and Swannington to see some dear friends who are exceptionally kind and generous to me. Also, I have a few other contacts in the area. I wish the town life, wealth, and prosperity renewed.

COALVILLE AS I REMEMBER IT -
Mrs Doris Roberts

I was born in 1902 in Wilkins Lane, Hugglescote, now Fairfield Road, the only child of John Andrew Jones and his wife, formerly Charlotte Clibbery. My mother, born in 1860, had been the 2nd eldest of a large family living on Ashby Road, Coalville. I remember her telling me of the time when she left home to go into service, like so many young girls in those days. She had left school (there was of course no free schooling in those days, it cast about 2d a week) and was 9 at the time. With her wicker basket containing a few belongings and her precious doll, she was sent off on the early morning milk train from Coalville to Leicester. She said this train was known as the "Dumilow" train, but I have no idea why. It would be about 1869 or 1870 and she went to a family in or near Leicester. There was much she did not like, especially a parrot which screamed and frightened her, so she saved up the little she earned and, without telling her parents first, caught the train back to Coalville and did not go away to service again. I believe she went back to school. The Schoolmaster's house was on Hermitage Road then. Later she went to work at Burgess's and held a good position there until she left when I was born.

My father was a miner and also Treasurer of the Manchester Order or Oddfellows. On Friday nights at our house, he would pay out the few shillings a week to those who had been off sick.

I loved Friday nights as mother and I always went to the market in Coalville. I felt proud of my mother who looked so smart wearing her black sealskin cape. We would walk down the middle of the road from Hugglescote; this would be 1908 to 1910. When we reached Oliver's crossing I often heard a hissing sound and asked her if a train was coming but it was a generator that Mr Lenton had to give him electricity, the first to have it in Coalville.

The lamp-lighter in Hugglescote was a familiar figure about that time, a Mr Woolerton, the father, or uncle I think, of the Mr Woolerton who became Head of Hugglescote School. At that time

The 'Red House' & Market Place. c1900s

58

he went around walking, with oil, matches, and a ladder, sometimes pushing his bicycle. Later he just had a long pole to pull on the gas street lights.

The market was on the corner where the 'Steam Packet' formerly the 'Red House' is. It was lively and exciting, with all the stall holders calling out their wares. The meat stalls faced the High Street, and meat would be auctioned there, almost on the steps of the 'Red House'. The Tylers lived at the 'Red House' then, their daughter Marjorie became Mrs Saunders, mother of John Saunders, producer of amateur shows.

On the path in front of the meat stalls were the stalls selling fruit, mainly apples, plums, and oranges. Oranges were 10 for 3d and there was one seller we called the "Orange King". There was also a "Rock King" who sold sweets. I don't remember vegetables for sale, I think most people grew their own. Sweets were penny a quarter, mainly hard fruit drops. Lucky bags were very popular.

ÇThe market went on until 11.00 p.m., which was also closing time for the shops. Many people were very poor in those days, and hung about until late, in the hope of being given meat that was beginning to decay, or fruit that was going rotten.

There were of course no cars about at this time, but farmers brought 8 to 10 folk at a time to the Market from Ibstock and Ellistown. These brakes did regular journeys, and one farmer, Mr Watson, eventually brought people in a landau.

Further along High Street, the market had very many second hand stalls which were always well patronised.

School Memories

I started school in 1907 at the school which is at the back of the Hugglescote Baptist Chapel in Dennis Street. Our teacher was Mrs Weston and Miss Lily Harris of Melbourne Street also taught us.

From Hugglescote Council School I won 3 scholarships, the County Ashby Girls' and Harley Foundation for Coalville. Mr Hatter of Hugglescote took me and the other Hugglescote entrant, Freda Deacon, later Mrs Onions, by trap to the small Harley Grammar School at Osgathorpe to take the exam. As train fares to Loughborough and Ashby were expensive, I went to Coalville.

At Coalville, on Forest Road where Newbridge is, Dr Storbest was the Head. During the 1914-18 war he had done Russian interpreting. After school he taught Russian to the first form 6. His brother, whom we called Dr John, taught maths and science. The senior mistress, Miss Alcock, was very strict. She lived on London Road near the 'Fox'. Mr Haddock (whom we called Fish!) had the use of the Phys. Lab. before the lab. at the Mining Institute, on the corner of Bridge Road and Avenue Road was built. He lived in the last house on the right in Charnwood Street, near the old Coalville East station, now demolished.

In 1920 or 1921 I started as a student teacher at Hugglescote New County Primary School where Mr Fellows was Head of Juniors and Mrs Weston Head of Infants. I started as a 'bursar' for two months with no pay, then was paid 9 pounds a month as a student teacher for a year. Later, in 1923, I went to Bridge Road where Mr Massey was Head of Juniors and Miss Lager Head of Infants. Arthur Newbury Choyce, our local poet and author, was Deputy Head there.

In 1927 I married Cecil Roberts and, under the Education Act of 1927, had to give up my job. Mr Massey tried to retain me but was not allowed to do so.

In 1928 I did some supply teaching at Ellistown Council School where children went from 5 to 14, the school leaving age. Mr Edwards, who had come from Snibston, was Head of Juniors and Mrs Underwood, who used to live at the house by the brook at the foot of Hugglescote Hill, was Head of Infants.

Other early memories

The only lamp lighter in 1908 or thereabouts was a Mr Woolerton of Ellistown. He went round with a ladder, oil, and matches originally, usually walking, but sometimes pushing his bike. Later, there were gas lamps, so he had a long hooked stick to pull on the gas chains. I was reminded of him when I was teaching by the poem "Leary, the Lamp Lighter" by R.L. Stevenson.

Hugglescote Church had very active bell ringers in those days. They practised a lot. The Band of Hope was also very active.

They used the old Hugglescote School room at the top of the Hugglescote Hill for their practice.

I always hated to see the pig-killer coming along. He was a Mr Cowley and had a scrubbed board on wheels which he used to push along. I hated to hear the pigs squealing so used to run indoors whenever I saw him. Many people kept their own pigs in those days so he was kept quite busy.

I also remember seeing the cattle being driven up the entry beside the butcher's shop opposite the 'Half Way House' in Central Road. I knew they were going to be slaughtered.

On Saturday mornings I often went to the barber's with my father. I enjoyed watching them shaving the men but was rather frightened of the cut-throat razors. The barber was opposite the wine shop in Belvoir Road which used to be Cross's Bakery.

Hugglescote and Ellistown Silver Band used to practise at the back of a house in Central Road, near the barber's.

Willn's Bakery was at Hugglescote where Thrush's is now. Joshua Willn's mother was a very strong character. As children we were a little nervous of her. She went around with a basket of bread, selling to local houses. Later they had a float and horse. I remember going to the shop with an empty jar to buy black treacle, which was sold loose then. Joshua's daughter, now Lily Harvey, worked very hard, both on the round and in the shop.

Another Saturday morning treat was to be taken by my father to the Olympia Skating Rink near Marlborough Square. A small band provided the music, I think this would be in about 1910. There were often fancy dress events there. I particularly remember the parents of Mr Wilkins, who owned and edited the Coalville Times, dressed in most effective half-black and half-white costumes. Mr Wilkins used to live on London Road, opposite Bakewell Street.

ODE TIMES - R.A. Roome

I can remember those dear childhood days
Those old fashioned folk with old fashioned ways
The top of Coalville with its solitary light
And that Iron clad man was a familiar sight
Lamplighter with ladder and hook on his pole
Firesides glowing with local hewn coal
Pit buzzer blowing three times a day
Telling the miners to be on their way
No unusual sight in this urban place
Was the collier going home with grime on his face

Pit Ponies at Snibston Pit. c1950s

The sight of pit ponies in the fields quite near
Brought up to graze just once every year
The hokey man standing outside Snibston Pit
and us with our Fridays penny clutched in our mitt
Short row and long row and down Bottom End
Down lanes and meadows our times we would spend
In the glass panelled tunnel we'd shelter from the rain
Or look up through the roof at some passing train
That brickyard pond where we bathed if we could
And come out all covered in red oily mud
We made our own pleasure and played our own games

62

Nicky Night and Tin a Lurky were a few of their names
Marbles and Whip and Top I think of once more
And the newspaper tablecloth we'd read before
Nineteen Twenty Six Strike I can recall
Those were the days we had nothing at all
In those dark days the only time we were fed
Was with a handout of soup and a crust of stale bread
The Miners went back without any rise
They couldn't defeat private enterprise
To earn a few coppers for jobs we would look
Like picking coal off the slag heap or collecting Hoss muck
Hands in our pockets for tuppence we'd grope
For a saucer of peas at the old "Band of Hope"
We'd get bulls eyes and sherberts, tiger nuts and pop
Locust and Lucky Bags from the little Corner Shop
"Nine o'clock Horses" will get you our parents would state
If we were apt to stay out too late
We searched at night and the horses we found
But it was only nightsoilers starting their round
So if you took short in the middle of the night
There were no indoor toilet where you could alight
At the bottom of the garden the old closet would stand
You'd set off with newspaper and candle in hand
We had air conditioning in those days of yore
With the wind blowing in under the door
Sitting there whistling and shuffling your feet
To scare any rats that were under the seat
The old Coalville Market with its parafin flares
Canvas topped stalls selling all kinds of wares
Goods all piled up for the people to see
And a tin clad shed where they sold jugs of tea
Those iron bridges over the colliery track
Little shunting engines with their trucks full of slack
Hotel and High Street and tree lined Marlboro' Square
The central field where we had our annual Fair
Co-operative bakehouse with its smell of new bread
Big railway sidings and large Loco shed

At the stores treat parade we'd follow the band
March round the town we thought it was grand
In a field all together from near and afar
We had sandwiches, cake and a small chocolate bar
As we grew up and in our early Teens
There were no sweat shirts or tight fitting jeans
But in sports coat and flannels all proudly arrayed
We strutted around on the Monkey Parade
Some Saturday nights we'd go to the flicks
Two seats on the back row for just three and six
Grange House and the Olympia and the Palais have gone
But the memory of these places still linger on
All Saints School is still standing there
Where we attended with lard plastered hair
Looking back over the years and the time that we had
I guess after all thay wonner tay bad.

MY CHARNWOOD - R.A. Roome

Adventure stirs within my breast
When I see Charnwood at its best
Old John standing there aloft
The ruins of Bradgate and Ulverscroft
Relics of those days of old
When fair maids rode with knights so bold
Ancestral home of Lady Jane Grey
Who lived there in King Henry's day
Now peacocks strut through cobbled arch
Where once the men at arms did march
The reservoirs still waters gleam
And Bradgates quiet meandering stream
Flanked by grassy banks and reeds
In sheltered spits the cray fish feeds
Mighty oaks where the ivy clings
Those little glades with fairy rings
That distant sound that we can hear
Is the coughing grunt of the fallow deer
Cattle graze where grass is lush

Their cloven hooves wild flowers they crush
To wander round those Charnwood rocks
Mid'st bluebells, broom and lady smocks
Growing there in wild abandon
Foxgloves, ferns and rhododendron
Woodhouse Eaves with its old world charm
The nature trails of Broombriggs Farm
Those familiar sounds that we all know
Wood Pigeon, Coot and Carrion Crow
Newly made mounds of turf and loam
Tells us of the voles new home
The sun rays beaming from on high
Help to ripen ears of wheat and rye
Rambling along on a summers day
And smell the scent of new mown hay
The beacon reaching for the sky
Where woodland birds and skylarks fly
To hear the cry of the screaming jay
And see bob-tailed rabbits at their play
Up in the rocks so stark and bare
An old red fox has made his lair
From the monastery built there in the dell
You can hear quite clearly its mournful bell
Booming out on the fragrant air
To summon the monks to midday prayer
Thats where you'll see an effigy
Of Jesus Christ on calvary
There in the outwoods not far away
The rare red squirrel has made his dray
Where pine boughs mingle overhead
And cones abound where ere you tread
Newtown Linford with its thatched abodes
Its quaint old shops and country roads
Nestling there in fields of green
The oaks in Charnwood can be seen
All these wonders that you can see
Are gifts from God and they are free

So, as the day draws to a close
I'll seek my bed and sweet repose.

THE ANCIENT MINER - R.A. Roome
Tramping through the darkened street
With hob nailed boots upon his feet
Along the road at a steady plod
The very road his sire had trod
Down the shaft or down the drift
Just another start to a working shift
Into the bowels of mother earth
With mining in his blood from birth
There where its eternal night
To search for coal by candle light
In a seam not three feet high
And the threat of danger always nigh
Creeping crawling hunched up there
Like some fearsome monster in its lair
Tattered trousers chest all bare
Breathing in that putrid air
Gnarled old fingers torn and sore
As at that precious coal he'd claw
Half blinded by the grime and sweat
The devils gold he had to get
Out into the gate from whence he came
Blinking in the candles flame
Then trying to get a bit of ease
With snap tin balanced on his knees
What have you got his mates would say
He answers same as yesterday
Squatting there upon the floor
He eats his snap from dirty paw
That old pit pony champs at its bit
And nuzzles round for his share of it
Up at last where there's bright blue skys
Hands held aloft to shield his eyes
Body wracked in a coughing bout

To try to get that coal dust out
At each weekend they all gather there
For the wages they all have to share
The miner looks at what he's been paid
And thinks of what is should have made
So with a sigh he turns his back
And sets off down that familiar track
There at the end of that well worn path
Is his own fireside and his old tin bath
Now gone are the moleskins the muffler and cap
The usual garb of a coal mining chap
No more in the fields will this man be found
With his ferrets and nets and his faithful old hound
A grand old man from the days of yore
Alas has gone and is no more
This man belonged to a special breed
Who lived by some unwritten creed
He's seen disasters, poverty and strife
All the hardships of a colliers life
For a century and a half this town has stood
Its roots planted firm in his sweat and blood
So in this year of our anniversary
Be justly proud of men such as he.

COALVILLE'S FIRST TELEPHONES-
Miss T.E. Stacey and Mr W. Stacey

When the Telephone Exchange was installed in 31 Park Road, Coalville, our parents Mr and Mrs W. Stacey were the caretakers, and our eldest sister Julia was the first operator, as near as we can say it would be in the year 1903.

When the exchange was opened there were only nine subscribers, two of them being the Police Station and Fire Station, and when we left in 1926 there were approximately 300.

Inside the front door of the house was a call box, in that day known as a silence box, because when anyone entered the box, the floor which was operated by two steel rods went down about an inch, making the box soundproof, while the person made the call. Years later telephone call boxes were erected in many parts, known as kiosks.

THINGS I HAVE SEEN HAPPEN IN COALVILLE SINCE 1904 -

A.F. Stinson

I can remember going to the old 'Grand' cinema as a boy, sitting on a board seeing a silent film called "The Broken Corn" an American Western. The words were printed on the screen. The cinema was owned by a Mr Johnson and it cost a penny to go in to see the film.

The Friday market was then held down one side of High Street and on the front of the Red House Hotel. The stall holders mostly came on the train from Leicester and they used to push their large baskets on wheels from the station at around 10.00 a.m. and not pack up until 10.00 p.m. at night. They lit the stalls by a paraffin lamp.

I can remember such characters as the "Orange King", the "Pot Man" and a butcher from Castle Donington, whose family still attend the Coalville market.

Another building called 'Olympia' was built for roller skating and this was then used for picture shows. The Salvation Army used to march down Belvoir Road on Sunday evenings at 6.00 p.m. and play around the gas lamp that was in the centre of the central crossroads. On the Ashby Road corner of this crossroads stood a First Aid hut and also an iron Gents' toilet. Behind this was waste land, fronted by a large board on which the Cinema advertised the weeks entertainment.

The Fair people used the waste land and further down Mantle Lane, before the underground road was made, the traffic went on the level and over a railway level crossing.

I remember Broom Leys School being used for Belgian refugees when they first came to Coalville, but they were later found houses in the area. Broom Leys House was then used as a convalescent home for soldiers from the 1914 World War. I used to transport them from the train in a Model T Ford. I took a party to Yarmouth in the Model T Ford, two trips there and back in the same day.

I had a driving licence when I was 14 years old. My father got it through Inspector Dobney who was in charge of the police at that time. We had the only hire car in the town for some time and I took a dance band to Coleorton Hall when Sir George Beaumont's son was one year old. I also remember taking a party to a Nottingham Test Match in 1921.

During the miners' strike of 1926, some of the miners started a shaft at the bottom of the Altons and used to wind up the coal in a huge basket by means of an old mangle. I went down the shaft to have a look round. Lorries used to come from Leicester to take back coal to the city. I remember taking the then Miners' Leader A.J. Cook around the district, and also the Liberal Leader Lloyd George coming to Coalville.

Coalville & District Miners' strike Support Group.

Mr Jack Smith of Ellistown, the local miners' agent, went down outh in an old gypsy caravan pulled by a horse, to raise funds or the miners.

I used to sell petrol out of 2 gallon cans before we had pumps. Ve had the first petrol pump in the district and a second one in 926. These were eventually replaced by electric pumps.

A Mr Clarke, who used to play the organ at Coalville Church, nd a Mr Jones of Bridge Road, both of whom were blind, tuned the pianos.

The Chapel at the top of Hotel Street was called Cave Adullam, which can still be seen over the top of the cycle shop window.

My father rented the ground where the Midland Red Garage now stands and we kept fowls and a garden there.

When I lived on High Street, I recall Mr New going up there at night with a horse and cart, collecting night soil.

The electric lights came to Coalville in 1925, and we sold the then Leicester and Warwick Company a motor cycle and side car, to help them deal with all the breakdown calls.

I remember the old parades Coalville had, and all the old English Fairs on Red House front. There was Whitford's, the

Temperance parade at the 'Gate Inn' Huggle scote.

pawnbrokers, Sitdown's the fruiterers, Henson's the butchers o Belvoir Road and Higgin's hairdressers and John Peace th fruiterers on High Street.

In those early days, Coalville had two cattle markets, one i Margaret Street and the other at the rear of the Red House.

Coalville Rugby Club started on a field on Broom Leys Road o the other side of the road to the present one. A Leicestershir County Show was held on the field where they now play.

I can say I have been on High Street nearly every day of m 78+ years.

THE COALVILLE I REMEMBER -
F.D. Whitmore

My memories of Coalville start from the 1920's. It was a totally different place to the modern town. My recollections seem to centre on cottages, small family business concerns, characters and a community spirit. It was a town that was recovering from the 1914 to 1918 war. A town that was slowly emerging from a crisis of money shortage, unemployment and low wages. A town that was going to be in the thick of things in the next crisis of the 1926 General Strike. Little did my childish mind foresee or imagine the kind of Coalville that was shaping up.

The east side of Coalville; London Road, Charnwood Street, Oxford Street, Cambridge Street, and just a small excursion to enter Bakewell Street and the tip at the back of a cobblers shop occupied by a Mr King, and Hills draper's shop, with the added adventure of playing around Coalville East railway station. These were the main areas of my childhood explorations.

However, my chance of learning about the big world of Coalville increased as my parents began to take me "down Coalville", it was always "down Coalville". These trips were mostly on a Friday. From the ivy covered cottages against the "Fox and Goose" hotel, our usual walk to Coalville would begin. My mother would point out the various places and people she was acquainted with. The vision of so many cottages is still with me.

London Road was full of big houses where most of the business people lived. The first row of cottages started just after the Church and what I later learned was the Church School. There was a small shop in the second row and then a cooked meat shop, the last one in the row. The small cottages each side of the "Leicester Hotel" and the characters that lived behind the small windows. Over the bridge, after having the monster belching flames, smoke and hundreds of sparks into the night sky, Woottons furnace pointed out, the magic of the shops began. Kemp's High Class grocery store, the ladies hairdresser, Wilsons little sweet shop, Parsons paper shop. On the opposite side was the Baptist Chapel, the smell of a fish and chip shop, then

71

Holmes printing to strike a chord. Grays the tailors, Harris and Son, family butchers, and a small row of cottages down a narrow opening. Then two smaller shops and Deacons Cafe, the row ended with Gutteridge Stationery and a drapers and clothing shop. Then another sweet shop, Turners, who eventually went into Belvoir Road and a family named Roberts took it over. Next to that was the Singer Sewing shop and Goodliffes furniture shop. Next to that was a three-cornered shop with an upstairs room that was turned into the Women's Labour Exchange. On walking across the level crossing of the old Midland Railway, on the left side was an old flour and cattle food mill. There was a railway siding that held two or three vans. There was a large drapery shop owned by a Mr Drewitt. In later years I found out that he was a benefactor to several local causes. His name is somewhere around the adult school. The public house 'Stamford and Warrington' was the next building with a kind of bridle path leading to one or two cottages down the side. After the path was a family business named Cramps who sold wine and newspapers among other things. I have a hazy memory of paint and wallpaper. There followed a whole conglomeration of shops with a small cafe called Hills just before the Midland Bank. The council chambers were above the bank. I think I could list them all but some stood out more than others. Guests the chemists, with its two huge bottles coloured green and red. A tailors shop with gas lighting, electricity still being in its infancy in the High Street. Lashmore's the jeweller, with more cottages at the rear, Browns shoe shop, with a small factory at the back that made hand made shoes and boots. A double fronted shop that Deacons eventually turned into the Midland Cafe. Later Hills purchased it and continued in that business. The Star grocery and general shop, the Maypole where the butter and margarine came in tubs and was then dealt with at the counter with wooden butter pats; every customer served individually. Lands the chemist, which was taken over by Timothy Whites. The name of Melias and Worthingtons Stores came to mind, also one or two private shops with a Mr Peacy and a Mr Starkey as owners. Then George Masons, Onions and Whites fish and poultry shop, a butchers

72

The 'Star Tea Co.' 1900

and Hawthorns, which has only just closed. Opposite the 'Greyhound' public house was the 'Red House' with its cobbled frontage, then the Times shop run by the Wilkins family. The Midland Cycle Company, Fryers the butchers, then more cottages with an opening leading to a blacksmiths shop. I remember the blacksmith but cannot recall his name. The 'Bluebell' public house, Marshalls Row of small cottages, then the 'Fountain' and Railway Row with the station master's house at the front, then the station itself. This was a busy place in those days. There was a small siding for loading and unloading, and I remember seeing circus animals and fair-ground equipment being unloaded, and then reloaded for the next journey.

As my excursions got a little more exciting I discovered different places on my own. Mammoth Street, Stone Row, and Club Row. I often wonder why the Church Army always started its crusades in these places. Were they really the biggest sinners?

What an exciting place the Penny Bazaar was when exploring Belvoir Road as far as the 'Grand' and Colemans shop. Being an adventurous little soul, I found my way to the Ebenezer Chapel, with its row of cottages at the back, but Ashby Road seemed to be all cottages. This was before the Midland Red came to the town. I have a very firm recollection of a 'charabanc', an open bus that travelled from somewhere against the Post Office. The 'charabanc' was painted yellow and its garage has recently been burnt down and is now demolished.

At this time there were changes taking place in what is now Memorial Square. The tower that was to be the town's War Memorial was completed in 1924. It was unveiled by the Hon. Mrs Booth from Gracedieu. The platform was on the 'new Market' side of the Square. I can very well remember all the flags covering the name stones falling in one go. It seemed like a touch of magic in my small mind. Somewhere along the line I remember a platform collapsing, but whether it was at the actual unveiling or a subsequent memorial service I am not sure. The tower was a big attraction that changed the centre of Coalville into an attractive square. However, the image of the old market sometimes known as the 'Red House' market and the red painted "New Market" on the opposite side did not change with the smoky paraffin flare lamps and leaky roofs. As we know, apart from changing to electric lights, there was little difference when it finally closed some years ago. The market people were well known characters. 'Marks the Orange King' who was forever chasing light fingered children from the back of the stall. Then a man who sold cheap watches, trinkets and bric-a-brac, he always entertained by producing watches from all over the place like a magician. The fruit and vegetable men were always trying to out-shout and outsmart each other. They loved Coalville market because of guaranteed trade from employees at Stablefords and the miners who were never 'skinny' with their money when they had it.

The month of August always seemed a busy month in the life of Coalville. There used to be the Coalville Flower Show held where the Municipal Offices now stand. There used to be speciality acts and demonstrations, apart from the flower and vegetable show. Fred Cox and his amusements were always in attendance, he always presented an organ recital on the Sunday night. Then there was the Hugglescote show, with its sports and cycle racing. The amusement people had a busy week rushing to Bardon for a one day wake, then to Hugglescote for another.

Then the big rush to Ravenstone Turn Co-op field for the biggest tea party in the world. The Co-op treat for about two thousand children who came from Ibstock, Heather, Whitwick, Thringstone, Snarestone and villages where there was a Co-op shop or bread round. The local train services were used to bring the hordes to the treat. The assembly point was Marlborough Square, and they paraded behind several bands, all carrying their mugs and their tickets for their bag of food. The younger ones used to have their mugs slung round their necks on a piece of string, and the final instruction they got from their parents was, "Dunna brek your mug or you wunna get a cup o' tea". The amusement people used to unleash gas balloons of animals and there was always a bandstand for entertainment. The Desford Boys Industrial School Band with their pill-box hats used to play, plus clowns and other entertainers. Oh! what a great day that was! Pat Collins amusements always came to a September Fair at the back of the new market. There were always two cycles hanging from the structure of the 'Dragons', a ladies and a gents cycle to be won. A local wit remarked that they were the same two hanging up every year. The story told was that Pat Collins always celebrated his daughter's birthday at Coalville, as she had been born here when the fair was on its summer tour. Coalville seemed to have a lot of fairs, another family named Holland Bros. always seemed to make a beeline for Coalville when they had no official fairs to fulfil. Their venue was mostly in Jackson Street on what was known as Colemans Field.

As I write this my mind wanders over some of the characters of Coalville. The Hawthorn brothers, one brother died in the early 1920s, but Edgar lived to a good age and lived with his sister on London Road. There was a Mr Noyes Jones, the music teacher, Harvey and Cecil Norris. Mr Frith, the headmaster, and Mr Clark the blind organist at Christ Church, who sold papers as a way of earning a living. It was uncanny how he could pick out the various books and papers from under his arm. Tit Bits had a green cover and I think Pearsons Weekly had pink cover, but he never hesitated to pull the Tit Bits out for my mother on a Saturday morning. Then there was the Rev. Pickbourne who preached at the 'Top Baptist'. The Kemp family, Josh on London Road, Frank the grocer just over the railway bridge, who traded from a former chapel known as 'Cave Adullam', the plaque can still be seen today above what is now a cycle shop. Another brother had the bakery on Belvoir Road, it was known as "Kemps Corner" and was always open on Christmas Day to cook poultry and joints for people. Of course they had to pay for the services. Mr Higgins the barber and cigarette merchant. Mr Peacy the grocer with his horse and dray. There were many tradesmen who sold from the horse and cart, mostly on a Friday or Saturday because nearly everyone was 'skint' the rest of the week. That was why the upper bracket had their 'Friday penny' and the lower classes their 'Saturday ha'penny' though in the case of the latter, it was not always guaranteed. Coalville East always seemed to attract activity. The Railway Station did a good trade with many girls and women going to and from work at Shepshed and Loughborough. Then the next morning the train would take a lot of students to Loughborough Art College. I can remember that they had to wear a very colourful uniform. My excitement consisted of trips from Coalville East and Whitwick. At that time the fare was 3d and penny ha'penny for children. There was always plenty of clanging and banging of railway wagons from the Spring Hill quarry and the coal sidings at the back of Whitwick Colliery, with its small siding for timber and other vans. The red Brooke Bond covered cart was always stationed somewhere close by. Eventually the Lyons Tea Co. took over, they had a small depot for many years. This line closed to passenger traffic in 1932.

The people who lived nearby were pestered nightly by 'spirit rapping', clattering tins and door knocking, even the tying together of two door knobs then banging both doors at the same time and running away like mad! Oh! how some families suffered this nightly torture on dark nights, mind you, one or two of the guilty were caught and reminded of their sins with a clout or a threat of boxed ears. These little gangs went very innocently to one anothers houses and when it was time to go home they were threatened with the "Ten o'clock horses" or even the "Nine o'clock horses" all depending on which pit hooter was going. The only time the pit hooters seemed in harmony was when they blew in the New Year and all the "horses" galloped together! Sometimes it was just the "Galloping horses", boy, did we gallop home. Other horses I can remember were the night soilers taking their loads away, then the market traders trotting back to Leicester on a Friday night. Mind you, it was usually to the 'Fox and Goose' to get their first pint. I learnt later that use was made of all the pubs between Coalville and Leicester. Somehow, I always associated Botts Hollow with the galloping horses. It was such a spooky place, with the wind in the trees, and just two oil lamps that kept blowing out. One did not stop long in that place on a dark and windy night. On odd occasions did we see the Fire Brigade with horses. Once, Spring Hill was on fire, and they made haste to get to that one. They had the assistance of one or two units of Territorials who were camping up there.

The 'Fox and Goose' field seemed to be a good centre of entertainment for sports and the odd carnival. The local football team, Coalville Swifts, and the Coalville Town Cricket Club, used the field for their activities. The Leicester County Cricket Club played matches on it in season. When that took place there was a high screen of hessian placed round the field in a bid to make people pay. Their efforts were not always successful as a lot of the locals knew the back way in. London Road United F.C. played close to. The Coalville Rugby Club which came into being about 1928 used the 'Fox and Goose' clubroom for changing and bathing. There were several spectacular Torch Light Tattoos when the Territorials were in camp on the Forest. Afterwards, the Coalville Horticultural Show moved their venue to that field when plans were developing for the municipal offices opposite the 'Leicester Hotel'. The crossroads at the 'Fox and Goose' was the scene of several accidents in the early days of motor cars, no halt, give way signs or traffic lights; no highway code. It was just free for all who got across first. Then someone, somewhere, had the idea of policemen on point duty.

The 1926 strike brought about a spirit of comradeship and community activities. The Adult School was used as a soup kitchen along with other places, the Co-op made up food parcels and tradesmen gave away different commodities. Oh what a melee when Sitdowns gave away crates of bananas. The strike also brought in its wake poverty, want, and debt, and the eventual closedown of Stablefords in 1928.

There was also a changing pattern of house building and road layout. The Avenue Road estate was in its infancy, as was the development of Forest Road, opposite Lindley's and Dr Jamie's house. There was dancing at the back of the park. Harry Hurd used to get one or two to lug his piano from his house. I think he was the first to set up a mobile Fish and Chip shop. We always knew when it was around by the black smoke and sparks flying from the tin chimney. At times he had black chips to match the smoke. Then there was Billy Burton and his "Chickabids" doing a bit of entertaining, all to help the strikers and their families keep their spirits and morale high. People could still smile and joke and maintain a community spirit even in the hardest times.

The closure of Stablefords in 1928 was another body blow to the life of Coalville. It threw hundreds of people out of work. The YMCA tin building was taken over as a men's labour exchange before the joint one was opened in Hermitage Road. The growth of Coalville was slowed down as it approached the '30s. Certain projects were started, perhaps to alleviate the problem. The Meadow Lane and Blackwood council houses were mooted, against opposition from private owners, who were building in what was supposed to be an upper class residential area. The Broom Leys cemetery was opened in the late twenties. I think the first person was buried there in 1927. The Coalville swimming baths were opened, again I think the year was 1932. There was still a period of depression, the miners worked a three day week, but even their lives were beginning to change with the opening of pit-head baths.

The year of 1935 was the Jubilee year of King George V and Queen Mary. Coalville made a good celebration. The main events were held in the 'Fox and Goose' field, but the biggest attraction was the bonfire on a field opposite the Forest Rock. I well remember sitting up there and watching the various torch light processions coming from different directions to join forces at the bonfire.

There did not seem to be much progress from that year until after the war. The old gas lamps were extinguished along with the brickyard kilns. The railways, factories, and dwelling houses were blacked out during the war. Bus loads of evacuees began to arrive from Birmingham and a few from London. Various firms connected with the war effort began to take up property to continue production. The town had a share of bombing but that is another story, perhaps to be told by a different generation to mine.

This sequence of events, shops and characters, does not necessarily follow in perfect order. It was just as memories flooded into my mind; one incident or person reminding me of another. Also certain family names have been left out as there are descendants still alive today. In conclusion the circle of progress from depression to a little prosperity is turning full circle. Is Coalville to return to the Twenties and Thirties? Perhaps in fifty years time a similar story of cottages, characters, and community spirit, will be written in the same kind of vein as the memories that I have committed to paper on the hundred and fiftieth anniversary of the Coalville I remember.

BRIEF COALVILLE MEMORIES -
Anon.

A particular memory from my childhood is the lamp-lighter doing his rounds. With his long pole, he would pull the chain to turn up the gas light on all the lamps. I believe he was a Mr Holt of Victoria Road; I think he had a crippled daughter Carrie.

Before the 1914-18 war, outings from Coalville were rare indeed; there was as much excitement about a visit to a place a few miles away as there would be in crossing the Atlantic today. A train ride to Loughborough was a real treat when I was 9 or 10. The seats I remember had cane backs on these early trains.

The annual Sunday School outing from Christ Church to Bradgate Park was an adventure indeed. We travelled by horse-drawn brake, first to High Tor Farm, for a picnic meal, and

79

then went on to Bradgate Park.

Much later, the buses began to run to Leicester. I think Birds owned the first of these. They had solid tyres, and did not give a smooth ride. I remember my parents having to stop the bus for me to be sick! Of course there were no bus stops at all; the bus picked up and put down wherever passengers wished.

The Miners' Bus.

I went to Christ Church, as did all my family. Mr Hosking was the Vicar; his daughter ran a small kindergarten on London Road and another daughter 'Nanny Hosking' was the district nurse. They were all very authoritarian. Mr Hosking was very high church. We sat in church for Sunday School and he would walk up and down the aisles and suddenly pounce on a pupil and ask her or him some questions on the bible. We all found this rather frightening.

MEMORIES OF COALVILLE -
Anon.

Mr Roughton and his daughter Edith had a lockup shop with bedroom over it in case they couldn't get home to Agar Nook on their bikes.

They were Quakers, and he lived with his wife and her sister in a cottage right near the brook at Agar Nook.

Mr.Roughton outside his shop. c1900

They were both fully qualified Chemists but, if the poorest of
people couldn't afford a doctor or to pay into a doctor's club, they
always prescribed herbal treatment over the counter. Most of the
herbs they grew themselves and they were always effective.

They kept goats at home, and never drank any other milk. The
sister Helen, was a children's Nanny, and travelled round Europe
a lot with different employers, but she developed arthritis and
was absolutely crippled. The only treatment she got for that was
sensible diet and a visit to a masseur at Tunstall three times a
year.

The mother spent her days walking for miles and handing
Plymouth Brethren Tracts to anyone handy. She finished her
days in agony, with gangrene in both legs, and still no doctor's
treatment.

Another uncle of mine was also a chemist, and worked for

81

Porter's shop, corner of Belvoir Road/Vaughan Street.
c1923

Porter's, opposite the police station. He opened his own busine:
as a wine and spirit merchant, and also sold newspapers ar
toys. Weston was the name, and his shop was directly opposi
the railway station. His children were some of the first pupils
Coalville Grammar School. They eventually went to live
Oadby.

Hotel Street. c1915